HEART OF THE ORDER

HEART OF THE ORDER

Baseball Poems

AN ANTHOLOGY

Edited, with an introduction by Gabriel Fried
Foreword by Daniel Okrent

A Karen & Michael Braziller Book
PERSEA BOOKS / NEW YORK

Persea Books, Inc.
277 Broadway, Suite 708
New York, New York 10007

Library of Congress Cataloging-in-Publication Data

Heart of the Order : Baseball Poems / edited, with an introduction by Gabriel Fried ; foreword by Daniel Okrent.—First edition.
        pages cm
"A Karen and Michael Braziller Book."
ISBN 978-0-89255-435-5 (pbk. with flaps : alk. paper)
1. Baseball—Poetry. 2. American poetry—20th century. 3. American poetry—21st century. 4. Baseball players—Poetry. I. Fried, Gabriel, 1974– editor of compilation.
PS595.B33H43 2014
811.008'0357—dc23
            2013041773

Designed by Rita Lascaro. Typeset in Georgia.
Manufactured in the United States of America
First Edition

For Archer Fried-Socarides, age 8 ¾,
the biggest Mets fan in the State of Missouri

CONTENTS

III. SANDLOTS AND CORNFIELDS

IV. EXPANDING THE STRIKE ZONE

V. SCREWBALLS AND DOUBLE PLAYS

VI. AT THE LETTERS

VII. GREATS OF THE GAME

FOREWORD

Although he certainly never wrote it down, perhaps Walt Whitman really did say, "I see great things in baseball. It's our game, the American game. It will repair our losses and be a blessing to us." This useful maxim was first cited by Horace Traubel in his nine-volume biography of his friend Whitman, and it has ever since been invoked whenever someone wants to exalt baseball's place in our national consciousness. Someone, for instance, like Annie Savoy, the literary-minded bombshell played by Susan Sarandon in *Bull Durham.* Annie also has another use for Whitman: she quotes his poems to seduce the Double A ballplayers who each season pass through her town (and her bed). "Have you heard of Walt Whitman?" she begins. "No," Nuke Laloosh replies. "Who's he play for?"

Annie might have been better served if she'd had a copy of *Heart of the Order* in hand. Nuke wouldn't have heard of any of these poets either—although plenty of them are very well known to people who actually read—but he would have instantly understood what inspires their poems. Poets write about baseball for the same reason they write about nightingales and urns; had he only had the chance to see Koufax pitch or Williams hit, Keats would have found both truth and beauty in our wonderful game.

Listen to Marianne Moore: "Writing is exciting/and baseball is like writing./You can never tell with either/how it will go. . . . "

So it is with the poems collected in *Heart of the Order*. They go everywhere. John Engels and William Trowbridge give us two different versions of the unathletic boy exiled to right field—Engels lost in the magical thinking of unrealizable dreams, Trowbridge peevishly spoofing his own ineptitude with an out-of-the-park last line. Donald Hall unreels the game's slow and stately rhythms to arrive at an elegy, while May Swenson's jumpy, staccato wordplay some-how takes us by poem's end to a confounding place just as apt. Gail Mazur inverts the usual trope and seems to determine that quotid-ian life is actually a metaphor for baseball. A pantheon of ballplayers appears here (Mays and Mantle, Josh Gibson and Satchel Paige), but so does a lineup of clay-footed mortals (Peanuts Lowrey! Ted Lepcio! Andy Seminick!). Plenty of fathers and sons, of course—and, in an excerpt from Edward Hirsch's poem "Siblings," a sister who, in a different time, might have been prouder of her precocious slider.

Hirsch played college baseball at Grinnell (the virtue of playing at the lowest collegiate level, he says, is that it enabled him to bat third in the order). Bruce Smith (who obliterates the florid, clichéd *faux*-poetry of "greened paradise" and "Newtonian symmetry" in his "Devotion: Baseball") actually had a tryout with the Phillies. Most of the others (though perhaps not Miss Moore) spent large chunks of their childhood years on sandlots or in Little League or chasing a walloped stickball down the Brooklyn streets. But all of these poets have spent hours and months and years doing the next best thing you can do with baseball—*thinking* about it.

Robert Francis may have thought about the game more than any of the others; apart from the natural world, it was possibly his most frequent poetic subject. In some of Francis's baseball poems, medium and subject are fused. They're poems about baseball, but they're also about poetry itself. One, "The Pitcher," is appropriately the very first poem in this volume, for it defines a communication between poetry and baseball that couldn't be clearer if you required radio announc-ers to conduct their play-by-play chatter in anapestic hexameter. For Francis, pitcher and poet are inseparable: "His passion how to avoid the obvious/His technique how to vary the avoidance./The others throw to be comprehended. He/Throws to be a moment misunderstood."

But—and this is important—only a moment.

DANIEL OKRENT
November, 2013

INTRODUCTION

When I was becoming a baseball fanatic in the early 1980s, tossing pop-ups to myself in rutty fields and following a dismal (and then, suddenly, formidable) New York Mets team, I always heard baseball described in poetic, even celestial language. At the age of seven or eight, I knew some poetry—William Blake, Emily Dickinson, Alfred Lord Tennyson—thanks mostly to a poetry-minded grade-school teacher. Even then I recognized the exquisite grandeur of Tennyson's fragment, "The Eagle," in the language I read and heard describing baseball: "He clasps the crag with crooked hands" could have described an at-bat by Johnny Bench. And those honeyed voices calling the play-by-play over my hand-held radio and our rabbit-eared television could have served as voices from "The Prelude": "The sun is shining, the sky is blue, it's a beautiful day for baseball," Bob Murphy would often begin his Mets radio broadcasts, with a childlike rapture and openness to the sublime worthy of Wordsworth. And though I could not yet identify the ecstatic populism of Walt Whitman (an early baseball enthusiast, by all accounts) in the sport's ubiquitous epithet, the National Pastime, I intuitively understood the figurative power of that phrase.

Baseball has always lent itself to all sorts of literature, more so than any other American sport. The reasons for this, it seems to me, may be derived at least in part from baseball's pacing: Within each contest, rhythmic lulls are punctuated by crackles of action, making it conducive to observation, reflection, transformation, and unpredictable drama. What's more, as has often been noted, Major Leaguers play virtually every day for six month seasons, giving them, even with their mindboggling salaries, a workmanlike quality in which stretches of failure are unavoidable; indeed, great players succeed less of the time in baseball than in any other team sport, and good teams win less, making it especially identifiable to hard-working fans. And of course baseball games are untimed (just as the summer days on which they're played can seem untimed), which offers up possibilities in a way that makes it particularly alluring as a setting for writers, including—perhaps especially—poets. Baseball's emphasis on lines and turns, on delivery and swing mark an unintended kinship to poetry; and its transition from a pastoral to urban to suburban pastime over the course of the twentieth century even seems to mirror (to me, at least) poetry's path through Modernism.

The poems in this anthology represent some of the very finest written about baseball that I've come across in many years of discovering and saving them. This is, in part, because most of them are not merely about baseball. In so many ways, these poets speak to our relationship to the past (individual and collective), to youth and promise, to senescence and mortality—yet they do so by engaging the most optimistic versions of our personal and national mythologies.

It's been noted that baseball is a team sport that highlights, sometimes mercilessly, its individual participants. It's not a game in which teams run plays with the intricacy or interdependence of football or basketball, and yet success in baseball is interdependent because a single player cannot be repeatedly featured: batters must hit in turn, ace pitchers compete just once every five games, and there is no "help defense" in which one fielder can counteract the deficiencies or mistakes of another. ("The ball finds you on defense," announcers often say about weak fielders.) To my ear, the poems in this book don't need any help; they star on their own. However, once assembled, they seem, like any great team, more than the sum of their parts; there is a vividness that runs across these poems, in addition to within them. For me, as an anthologist, there is a particular pleasure in bringing together illustrious names like William Matthews and Marianne Moore with rising stars like Sarah Gridley.

(In baseball, beloved older players give way to their successors; in poetry, it needn't be so.)

As with the assembly of any roster, this one is noteworthy for its cuts as well as for those who made the team. There are, certainly, exceptional poets and poems that we overlooked or could not include for one reason or another. I feel I should acknowledge the exclusion of perhaps the two most famous baseball poems ever written, Ernest Thayer's "Casey at the Bat" and Franklin Pierce Adams' "Baseball's Sad Lexicon" (often known by its refrain of "Tinkers to Evers to Chance.") Simply by mentioning these two poems in this introduction, I suspect that I conjure them to mind sufficiently for many readers. Both are Hall of Fame poems, implicitly a part of this anthology in their spirit and influence.

"I know the announcer's not a rabbi or sage," writes Gail Mazur in one of her two extraordinary baseball poems in *Heart of the Order*. Even if we know that, too, for many of us baseball provides a sort of spiritual base, an oral tradition, a written and unwritten scripture. Although, as Mazur writes elsewhere, "the game of baseball is not a metaphor and [we] know it's not really life," sometimes it feels like an unmistakable facsimile for who we are and how we'd like to be—we'd *like* it to be a metaphor for our lives, even if it cannot always be, quite. But reading these poems, with their poignancy, eloquence, and music, their engagement with our longings and sense of nostalgia, it does feel awfully close.

I hope you enjoy these poems as much as I do—that they conjure for you the grace and grit of baseball, its simple elegance and complexity, in ways both familiar and wholly new. I hope, too, that the book reaches some fans who don't typically read poetry—and some poetry readers who don't (yet) care for baseball. If this intersection of these two loves of mine brings together fans of one camp into that of the other, it will further underscore to me that the poets in the book are hitting home.

GABRIEL FRIED

I.

Baseball Fundamentals

ROBERT FRANCIS

The Pitcher

His art is eccentricity, his aim
How not to hit the mark he seems to aim at,

His passion how to avoid the obvious,
His technique how to vary the avoidance.

The others throw to be comprehended. He
Throws to be a moment misunderstood.

Yet not too much. Not errant, arrant, wild,
But every seeming aberration willed.

Not to, yet still, still to communicate
Making the batter understand too late.

JOSEPH STANTON

Catcher

For Tim McCarver

The dove must fly straight to the heart,
the place you have prepared with pain—
your crooked hand swollen that the strike
might live. You kneel for the reliever,
as he frets his small golgotha,
his mound of grief. Eyes pleading with sky,
he's nailed to the cross of his failing
fastball and hanging curve. You lean
before to show the way the ball

must go. Baptist of never ending
perspiration, you must serve up—
again and again and again—
your head upon the plate where
the umpire of all he surveys
may fail once more to save your life,
while all eyes follow the lurid feet,
the batter's prance of twitch and stretch,
leading to what might be the dance
that makes your martyrdom complete.

DAVID BOTTOMS

Sign for My Father, Who Stressed the Bunt

On the rough diamond,
the hand-cut field below the dog lot and barn,
we rehearsed the strict technique
of bunting. I watched from the infield,
the mound, the backstop
as your left hand climbed the bat, your legs
and shoulders squared toward the pitcher.
You could drop it like a seed
down either base line. I admired your style,
but not enough to take my eyes off the bank
that served as our center-field fence.

Years passed, three leagues of organized ball,
no few lives. I could homer
into the garden beyond the bank,
into the left-field lot of Carmichael Motors,
and still you stressed the same technique,
the crouch and spring, the lead arm absorbing
just enough impact. The whole tiresome pitch
about basics never changing,
and I never learned what you were laying down.

Like a hand brushed across the bill of a cap,
let this be the sign
I'm getting a grip on the sacrifice.

ROBERT FARNSWORTH

Night Game

Nobody's just watching, not those perched
on a billboard beyond the center-field fence,
not the paid attendance, not the manager
thinking through his roster in the dugout,
slowly clapping. In a verdant block of light
carved out of evening, the game patiently
proceeds to discover its own dimensions.
Across the diamond, beyond the upper deck,
huge glass towers sheer into darkness.

Joy will make waves in thousands of people.
Lesser occasions—sudden fouls, foreign
scores, chin music—register on the crowd's
broad face like smiles donated to keep up
conversation. Two pale clouds have anchored
near the flag, whose broad stripes swell
and then subside. In the press box shirtsleeved
men look on like admirals from a bridge,
translating each habitual scuffing of spikes
or cap adjustment into megahertz of tension.

The pitcher stalks behind the mound, kneading
the ball, wiping his brow with a forearm.
A gentle wish of blue smoke hangs over his head.
At last he leans in, like one admonishing a child
who has stumbled into trouble he might have
avoided. Precision richly mixed with accident
has left two on, two out, two-nothing for

the home team in the ninth. Gull shadows flicker
over the poised infield. As he begins his toppling
stride, the pitcher reaches into his glove,

plucking as out of a hat the ball and slings it
suddenly home. And it is emphatically
reversed, rising into the lights, into darkness.
In the bat's risen arc of follow-through
there's an instant nobody solves, not the hitter
already shedding his weapon and starting
to run, not the pitcher strangely dancing down
to back up the plate. The center fielder trots back

and turns, spreading his capable arms open in greeting.

Edwin Rolfe

Kill the Umpire!

He's the infallible man:
calm, caller of balls and strikes,
hits and errors, fair and foul.
He tells us when we're safe or out.

Each of us desires his favor.
Each has his enemy, his chosen side.
We need not only the big battalions
of bats, but also the aid of God.

And he is God. We worship him when
his word delights our partisan eyes.
But when his justice moves the other way,
we rage, we fume, we shout for his blood.
We would follow him home, if we could, through swarming
streets, through alleys, suburbs, country lanes,
creep up on him from behind and kill him—bang!—
with a pop-bottle. We always kill God.

But since we cannot get him, we're content
to kill him in our thoughts, to shout
Unfair! Unfair! Buy him a pair of glasses!
He's blind as a bat! But the game goes on
according to its rules, which he upholds
by eye, by arm, by his called decision.

Each game has its own peculiar laws
and each its own direction, history;
and he who calls the critical turns
is a lonely man, a man without a country,
a prophet without honor in his own land.

We who sit on the grandstand, watching
the home team lose the heart-breaking close ones,
revile him, damn him—the solitary man—
stare at him, dressed in black like a judge,
his face encased in the steel-wired mask,
the eyes behind it steady, wise;

fearing, knowing the outcome, yet
powerless to prevent the sure defeat.

We sit and watch in outraged silence.
We hate him because whatever he says is true.

MAY SWENSON

Analysis of Baseball

It's about
the ball,
the bat,
and the mitt.
Ball hits
bat, or it
hits mitt.
Bat doesn't
hit ball, bat
meets it.
Ball bounces
off bat, flies
air, or thuds
ground (dud)
or it
fits mitt.

Bat waits
for ball
to mate.
Ball hates
to take bat's
bait. Ball
flirts, bat's
late, don't
keep the date.
Ball goes in
(thwack) to mitt,

and goes out
(thwack) back
to mitt.

Ball fits
mitt, but
not all
the time.
Sometimes
ball gets hit
(pow) when bat
meets it,
and sails
to a place
where mitt
has to quit
in disgrace.
That's about
the bases
loaded,
about 40,000
fans exploded.

It's about
the ball,
the bat,
the mitt,
the bases

and the fans.
It's done
on a diamond,
and for fun.
It's about
home, and it's
about run.

CAROLE OLES

The Interpretation of Baseball

It took time to study who was missing
from the dream ball club that paraded
through the dark in uniforms and numbers
holding up posters of the lost teammate
as if campaigning for their man.

I had to walk the dream railroad track again
where my son followed me at first, then took
the lead, balanced, leaped forward over the ties,
poof—gone.
And to sit with the inquisitor who wore
my dachshund around his neck like a precious
fur with lacquered eyes.

I had to listen then to memory,
your fastball, your grand slams out of the park.
And go back to the bleachers at Yankee Stadium
where you took me at 7 though I was not the son
whose heart, that sly courser, unseated him.
He was the one you saved your prize for,
the baseball Babe Ruth signed.
At the game you tried to show me what you saw
but I was gabbing about something else:
another hot dog, how many more minutes.

It took time, Father, to see
you swinging, connecting.

Ronald Wallace

Fielding

I like to see him out in center field
fifty years ago, at twenty-two,
waiting for that towering fly ball—
August, Williamsburg, a lazy afternoon—
dreaming how he'd one day be a pro
and how he'd have a wide-eyed son to throw
a few fat pitches to. An easy catch.
He drifts back deeper into a small patch

of weeds at the fence and waits. In a second or two
the ball is going to stagger in the air,
the future take him to his knees: wheelchair,
MS, paralysis, grief. But for now
he's camped out under happiness. Life is good.
For at least one second more he owns the world.

MILLER WILLIAMS

Catch with Reuben

You took for gospel what I said,
holding the glove
in just the way I said you should.
Knowing I never could teach you enough,
I thought that when you understood
how carelessly moments disappear,
your mind might hold, from a distant year,
a fading day and us still here.

No matter that your legs are short,
your arms are small,
it will all be right in time.
This arm that never threw a ball
far enough to make a team
if more than nine came out to play
threw one into your hands today
from nearly sixty years away.

J.T. Barbarese

Teaching the Slider

In the middle of life's road, which I notice
keeps getting wider,

he asks me to show him a slider.
Bankrupt, filled with rage, and now caught

on the phone with a merciful woman who isn't his mother,
I slam the phone down,

order him to the backyard,
and pitch. *Don't push off, separate*

because it's how you separate yourself from the mound,
it's all in the follow-through.

I come straight over the top.
They break smoothly, cleanly.

Once I broke them off and they fell
like knives outlining my victims.

Baseball's a game played sideways, I say.
He tries, is all legs and arms. His hands

half the span of mine, sneaks untied,
he's a present coming unwrapped. *No,*

you're not coming all the way through.
You need to fall through your body

as if it weren't there. You need to plunge
down the steps your legs and back make

and then the ball will break
and fall off the end of the world

no matter what and after that
your body can burst into flames

for all I care and I come through
and the ball cracks his glove, knocks it off.

JONATHAN HOLDEN

A Personal History of the Curveball

It came to us like sex.
Years before we ever faced the thing,
we'd heard about the curve
and studied it. Aerial photos
snapped by night in *Life*, mapping
Ewell "The Whip" Blackwell's sidearm hook,
made it look a fake: the dotted line
hardly swerved at all.
Such power had to be a gift
or else some trick; we didn't care which.
My hope was on technique.
In one mail-order course in hypnotism
that I took from the back-cover
of a comic book, the hypnotist
like a ringmaster wore a suit,
sporting a black, Errol Flynn mustache
as he loomed, stern but benign
over a maiden.
Her eyes half-closed, she gazed
upward at his eyes, ready
to obey, as the zigzag strokes
of his hypnotic power, emanating
from his fingertips and eyes,
passed into her stilled, receptive face.
She could feel
the tingling force-field of his powers.
After school, not knowing
what to look for, only

that we'd know it when it came—
that it would be strange—
we'd practice curves, trying
through trial and error to pick up by luck
whatever secret knack a curveball took,
sighting down the trajectory
of each pitch we caught
for signs of magic.
Those throws spun in like drills
and just as straight,
every one the same.
In Ebbets Field I'd watch
Sal "The Barber" Maglie train
his batter with a hard one at the head
for the next pitch,
some dirty sleight of hand down and away
he'd picked up somewhere
in the Mexican League. Done,
he'd trudge in from the mound.
His tired, mangy face had no illusions.
But the first curve I ever threw
that worked astonished me
as much as the lefty cleanup man I faced.
He dropped, and when I grinned
smiled weakly back. What he'd seen
I couldn't even guess
until one tepid evening in the Pony League
I stepped in against a southpaw,

a kid with catfish lips
and greased-back hair,
who had to be too stupid
to know any magic tricks. He lunged,
smote one at my neck.
I ducked. Then, either
that ball's spin broke every law
I'd ever heard about or else
Morris County moved almost
a foot. I was out
by the cheapest trick the air
can pull—Bernoulli's Principle.
Like "magic," the common love songs
wail and are eager to repeat
it helplessly, *magic*, as if to say
what else can I say, it's magic,
which is the stupidest of words
because it stands for nothing,
there is no magic. And yet
what other word does the heartbroken
or the strikeout victim have
to mean what cannot be and means what is?

JAMES POLLOCK

Radio

The kitchen dark, the summer night air warm,
And my father at the kitchen table, radio

Turned down low, alone, listening to baseball.
My mother and I come inside from our swim,

Toweling off. The crowd is restless. Long silences
Between pitches in the play-by-play.

Look how he holds the radio in both hands
Like a steering wheel, thumb on the tuning dial

To catch the wavering channel, fighting static.
His eyes glitter like a field of fireflies.

DONALD HALL

The Baseball Players

Against the bright
grass the white-knickered
players tense, seize,
and attend. A moment
ago, outfielders
and infielders adjusted
their clothing, glanced
at the sun and settled
forward, hands on knees;
the pitcher walked back
of the hill, established
his cap and returned;
the catcher twitched
a forefinger; the batter
rotated his bat
in a single circle. But now
they pause: wary,
exact, suspended while
abiding moonrise
lightens the angel
of the overgrown
garden, and Walter Blake
Adams, who died
at fourteen, waits
under the footbridge.

II.

Stickball, Pickle, and Little League

John Meredith Hill

April

There are puddles.
        If a person wanted to
                he could spend an hour

picking up litter,
        raking, mowing
                tufts of grass.

A white cloud hangs high
        in the sky down
                the third base

foul line. One boy arrives
        & then another &
                another & another.

WILLIAM TROWBRIDGE

Poets' Corner

They put me in right field
because I didn't pitch that well
or throw or catch or hit,
because I tried to steer the ball
like a paper plane, watched
Christmas gifts with big
red ribbons floating through
the strike zone, and swung
at dirt balls. So they played the odds,
sent me out there in the tall grass
by the Skoal sign, where I wandered
distant as the nosebleed seats
my father got us in Comiskey Park,
my teammates looking
remote and miniature,
their small cries and gesticulations
like things remembered
from a dream. I went dreamy,
sun on my face, the scent
of sod and bluegrass, the lilt
of birdcall and early cricket
bending afternoon away
from fastballs and hook slides
to June's lazy looping
single: baseball at its best,
my only fear the deep fly
with my name on it,
meteoric as Jehovah

or Coach Bob Zambisi
closing in to deliver once
again the meaning of the game:
what it takes to play, why I had to
crouch vigilant as a soldier
in combat, which he never
had the privilege of being,
and stop that lolling around
with my head up my ass,
watching the birdies and picking
dandelions like some kind of
little priss, some kind
of Percy Bitch Shelby.

JOHN ENGELS

Night Game in Right Field

Lord, but that ball would rise
high in the flare of the lights
become like something always there,
round, full, shining little moon,

float longer than it should,
and then decline to exactly where
I ought to have found myself
camped under it, casual, easy

—instead, scared
and staring blind into the lights,
born to retribution of mismeasure,
I always froze, my last hope luck,

or absent luck, then somehow
revelation, would pray
that this one time, just this once,
I might know exactly where

on the field to set myself, might
reckon rightly the convergences, hot glove
waiting, ready to make
the play, lovingly to gather in

that elegant curve
of the falling into place.

DAVID LIVEWELL

Stickball at St. Mike's

We strained to follow hits to the top story.
The traceries were triples, grounders strikes.
A homer had to clear the slated pitch.

Like Michael's sword, our broomstick swung at strikes,
As the church tower's shadow draped each pitch
And evening dimmed Good Friday's stained-glass story.

All but the dusk was fair. Then, black as pitch,
The sky obscured our vision and His story
Of a thrust spear and jagged lightning strikes.

A final pitch, three strikes. . . . That game is history.

THOMAS LUX

The Man into Whose Yard
You Should Not Hit Your Ball

each day mowed
and mowed his lawn, his dry quarter-acre,
the machine slicing a wisp
from each blade's tip. Dust storms rose
around the roar, 6 p.m. every day,
spring, summer, fall. If he could mow
the snow he would.
On one side, his neighbors the cows
turned their backs to him
and did what they do in the grass.
Where he worked, I don't know,
but it set his jaw to: tight.
His wife a cipher, shoebox tissue,
a shattered apron. As if
into her head he drove a wedge of shale.
Years later, his daughter goes to jail.
Mow, mow, mow his lawn
gently down a decade's summers.
On his other side lived mine and me,
across a narrow pasture, often fallow—
a field of fly balls, the best part of childhood
and baseball. But if a ball crossed his line,
as one did in 1956,
and another in 1958,
it came back coleslaw—his lawnmower
ate it up, happy

to cut something, no matter
what the manual said
about foreign objects,
stones, or sticks.

BILL MEISSNER

Summer of 1963: The Orbit of the Wiffle Ball

It didn't matter that the wind
blew your high pop-ups back to home plate,
didn't matter that a hard line drive stopped dead
in the thick grass.
You just kept swinging the bat, believing the ball
would fly farther than it ever did.
You stared at the Wiffle ball, a tiny moon with holes in it,
and thought about John Kennedy on his inauguration,
speaking into the holes of a microphone.

Each time you connected, you
clacked the ball toward your house,
toward windows it could not shatter.
You and your friends were just kids,
and you swore you'd stay that way
forever. You ran the bases each day
until you wore a dirt path in
your fathers' patience,
until your mothers swung open the screen door,
and you slid into home for dinner.

Unbreakable, the cardboard Wiffle ball box claimed.
But the white plastic cracked after two weeks of batting,
so you returned it to the Ben Franklin store for a new one.
Walking proudly on the buckled sidewalk, you turned
the new ball over and over, imagining you
held the whole world in the palm of your hand.

In August, you stood alone in your yard at dusk,
not realizing how cold the winds would be in November.
Your bat perched like a rifle on your shoulder,
you braced yourself as the breeze picked up, the national anthem
caught in your ear,
your pants wrapping and unwrapping around your ankles
like flags.

That summer all you could think about was
tomorrow, how high you could hit a Wiffle ball
when your arm muscles turned eighteen.
You'd send it flying all the way to the moon.
The future was out there
like a pop fly dropping from space,
and you'd be waiting for it—your small, growing hands
outstretched,
your faith unbreakable.

Hitting Fungoes

Hitting fungoes to a bunch
of kids who asked me
nicely, I'm afraid the hard
ball they gave me might
shatter the stained-glass
window of the church
across this abandoned lot.
I see it all now, in
the moment the ball leaves
my hand before it smacks
the bat: we scatter
in every possible direction,
but the pastor, sensing
a pervert, screams
to the cops to chase
the big one, and there
I am: trapped. I pull
my old Woodrow Wilson
Fellowship Letter out
of my worn suit pocket,
wave it wildly, but they
smell last night's sex
on my breath, condemn
me to jail for failure
to escape my terror of failure
itself. I swing without
thinking, the only way,
and the crack

is a heretic's hip-bone
ripped from its socket
on the rack. Not bad.
Not too deep, but a nice
arching loft. One kid,
who runs faster than the others,
makes a spectacular
diving catch and throws it back.

STUART DYBEK

Clothespins

I once hit clothespins
for the Chicago Cubs.
I'd go out after supper
when the wash was in
and collect clothespins
from under four stories
of clothesline.
A swing-and-a-miss
was a strike-out;
the garage roof, Willie Mays,
pounding his mitt
under a pop fly.
Bushes, a double,
off the fence, triple,
and over, home run.
The bleachers roared.
I was all they ever needed for the flag.
New records every game—
once, 10 homers in a row!
But sometimes I'd tag them
so hard they'd explode, legs flying apart in midair,
pieces spinning crazily
in all directions.
Foul Ball! What else
could I call it?
The bat was real.

The Baserunner

We stood in that thick light of late day
throwing the ball down the sidewalk,
playing "Pickle," the game of stolen bases,
arms flinging the ball away like a thing
you had to get rid of, the splat in the mitt
resounding off the porches and doors
of houses lining the street, as shadows
of trees grew long and the sun sparked
in the eyes of the boy facing west, until
at last we saw in the dance of the runner,
the lifted foot, the swung shoulder
dodging the deft tag, a motion coalesce
like mist on evening lawns, touched
by grace, tied up with time and carried
through the years to the present where,
eyes closed against the light, I see
the solemn joy of him, a character
of fiction and unbounded love.

EDWARD HIRSCH

from Siblings

That small southpaw rocking forward on the mound
And scowling at a right-handed batter coiled in the box
In front of a stubby catcher calling for the pitch

Is my sister Lenie trying out for Little League
On a mild Sunday afternoon in mid-July, 1959.
I remember the triumph and exaltation

Of her blistering fastball rising at the knees
And her curveball nicking the corners at the waist
And her high off-speed changeup at the letters

That sent a string of cocky twelve-year olds
Back to the dugout shaking their heads in wonder
At a girl piling up strikeouts against them.

But my sister only remembers the humiliation
Of striking out so many older boys in a row
While their fathers gathered on the infield grass

And tried to persuade my stubbornly determined dad
That using a girl on the mound was against the rules,
All the while marveling at her masterful control.

The men in our family were proud of my sister's
Precocious slider and sloping curveball,
Her slow windup and sneaky whip-like quickness,

The way she mixed up her stuff and concentrated
On the target stationed on the outside corner,
Reaching inside herself for her best pitches.

But it wasn't until I listened to Lenie
Telling the story to a cousin twenty years later
At a Sunday afternoon picnic in Ravinia Park

That I understood how much she hated the memory
Of toeing the rubber and reducing so many older boys
To silence, their bats waving uselessly in the air. . . .

The story of siblings is the story of childhood
Experienced separately and together, one tree
Twisting in different directions, roots and branches,

One piece of land divided up into parcels,
Acres and half-acres, parts of a subdivision,
Memories carved into official and unofficial versions.

SHARON OLSON

Running the Bases

The first-base coach tells her to run on anything.
The third-base coach smiles, says, *how did you get here?*

The journey had been effortless
because she really did not remember running,
as if she had not paid attention to detail, again.

She dared not look back,
the runners were piling up behind her, one by one.
The opposing team members were eager to embrace her,
and she could feel herself tempted by comfort, and betrayal.

But her father and brother, standing outside the bases,
had guided her this far, and she felt nothing
like debt, or honor, only warmth, as if
the words and the smile were more than a gesture:
Listen to us, they said, *and you will be safe
no matter what happens, for you have learned
about the journey you will make to the riverside
where the boat is waiting, the arms around you,
the final letting go.*

*In this moment, look around you at this outfield,
this infield, write down what you remember
before you leave to come home.*

Spring Baseball

Pine trees envy
the wind's liberties

so sway sometimes
on a still day.

A small boy wears his
brother's baseball cap.

LARRY MOFFI

Homage to a Vacant Lot

Mr. and Mrs. Davies live upstairs.
He follows the Dodgers. She follows
him. She works for Aetna, he
for The Travelers. They do what
nobody bothers to ask, the paperwork
of other people's lives in offices
where colleagues are legion.
Twice each summer they go off on her
Company sponsored trip, or his, cardboard
Valise holding them up on the corner
until the blue tobacco bus takes them
away: Boston, a long weekend.

Otherwise, he drinks beer and smokes
five solid months on the porch,
Brooklyn on the radio, the mourning
of the pennant race. Drunk, especially
drunk, he dispenses his portion of
wisdom, the philosophy of the all-important
loss column, "losses being what kill you,
you can make up a win but never a loss."
Or else I am shagging flies he lifts
high across the vacant lot. "Two
hands!" he shouts, "Two hands!" And I try.

III.

Sandlots and Cornfields

JAMES APPLEWHITE

Home Team

There was a stillness about the games, afternoons,
        something to be decided, but in suspension—a runner
taking his lead as the pitcher eyed him suspiciously,
        the outfielders glancing back at the bushes thirty
feet to their rear, edging in a little, trying to remember
        the soft spots, where a line drive wouldn't bounce up.
Thunderheads building in the sky enveloped the scene within
        an elemental light. The thickening, varnishlike quality
of water in air, and heat—the pure clarity beginning to
        congeal—would capture this space at the edge of a village,
gathering the figures into one impression, while a fly ball
        hit long toward right center hung up against the base
of a cloud, the crowd rising to its feet as the runner on first
        broke joyously for second, toward home. Charlie Boykin,
coming around the bases, grinned with the mouths of small boys
        under the tree, their biceps thicker as they looked at his.
So the game and those summers continued. But Charlie Justice
        played for the Redskins, his figure ghostly in the electronic
snow of TV—not on a field near the one that Willie
        Mozingo had plowed, before he took his chunky body into
far left field, a two-legged gleam in his cream-colored uniform,
        as afternoon deepened and the slanting sun made balls hard
to judge but he caught them anyway, back in the broom sedge.
        Fred Pittman signed the minor-league contract and people
went to Wilson to see him. The diamond was left to high-
        school games, to frog creak and owl whoop in midsummer
evenings, and the lightning bugs coming on in a space that
        held the stars. Houses in the sight of the diamond oak

lit up their windows with the glow of TV. Always a few
    farm boys, not risking injury, hit rocks toward the trees
with broomsticks, or prevailed on a younger brother to throw
    them one more pitch down the middle, so they could drive
the baseball over the weeded ditch, out of the pasture.

YUSEF KOMUNYAKAA

Glory

Most were married teenagers
Working knockout shifts daybreak
To sunset six days a week—
Already old men playing ball
In a field between a row of shotgun houses
& the Magazine Lumber Company.
They were all Jackie Robinson
& Willie Mays, a touch of
Josh Gibson & Satchel Paige
In each stance & swing, a promise
Like a hesitation pitch always
At the edge of their lives,
Arms sharp as rifles.
The Sunday afternoon heat
Flared like thin flowered skirts
As children & wives cheered.
The men were like cats
Running backwards to snag
Pop-ups & high-flies off
Fences, stealing each other's glory.
The old deacons & raconteurs
Who umpired made an *Out* or *Safe*
Into a song & dance routine.
Runners hit the dirt
& slid into homeplate,
Cleats catching light,
As they conjured escapes, outfoxing
Double plays. In the few seconds

It took a man to eye a woman
Upon the makeshift bleachers,
A stolen base or homerun
Would help another man
Survive the new week.

Richard Hugo

Missoula Softball Tournament

This summer, most friends out of town
and no wind playing flash and dazzle
in the cottonwoods, music of the Clark Fork stale,
I've gone back to the old ways of defeat,
the softball field, familiar dust and thud,
pitcher winging drops and rises, and wives,
the beautiful wives in the stands, basic, used,
screeching runners home, infants unattended
in the dirt. A long triple sails into right center.
Two men on. Shouts from dugout: go, Ron, go.
Life is better run from. Distance to the fence,
both foul lines and dead center, is displayed.

I try to steal the tricky manager's signs.
Is hit-and-run the pulling of the ear?
The ump gives pitchers too much low inside.
Injustice? Fraud? Ancient problems focus
in the heat. Bad hop on routine grounder.
Close play missed by the team you want to win.
Players from the first game, high on beer,
ride players in the field. Their laughter
falls short of the wall. Under lights, the moths
are momentary stars, and wives, the beautiful wives
in the stands now take the interest they once feigned,
oh, long ago, their marriage just begun, years
of helping husbands feel important just begun,
the scrimping, the anger brought home evenings
from degrading jobs. This poem goes out to them.

Is steal-of-home the touching of the heart?
Last pitch. A soft fly. A can of corn
the players say. Routine, like mornings,
like the week. They shake hands on the mound.
Nice grab on that shot to left. Good game. Good game.
Dust rotates in their headlight beams.
The wives, the beautiful wives are with their men.

Game Day

Coal man who lowers a tin channel
like a playground slide through cellar windows
then hunches under a canvas basket,
he's come home, a stop on his route,
and what is he to make of his only son?
"What are you doing here?" the father
roars, leaning across the kitchen table,
thick fingers splayed. "What are you doing here?"
The boy doesn't know how to answer,
staring at those hands, but he's in fifth grade
and no one's going to make him cry.
At school he worked a case of fake chills
into a permission slip and came home
—his mother won't be back till supper—
to make lineups from baseball cards,
every player backed by his stats.
They're waiting in kitchen sunlight, stars
in sugary dust of the chewing gum
that comes with them. "Speak to me,"
the father says again, not moving his hands
from the table where at meal time
he speaks to no one. The boy's stomach
is quicksand as though he's watching from
the on-deck circle or kneeling again
in the confessional for the first time.
Last week his team visited the orphanage,
and after the game—he won it with a single—
while new friends were all having Kool-Aid

in the dining hall, he closed his eyes and wished
he could live in the home for boys.
He won't say anything, staring at the table.
A twenty-game winner goes into his windup.
What can the father do now but turn
and fill the cellar bin, then go on with
his route, leaving handprints of coal?

David Clewell

from Heroes

Friday nights the town eats early.
Lights flood the field and bleachers fill
with people cheering themselves on.
Any team from out of town
is good enough to lose.
The taste of sweat at lip's curl
is enough, reminds them
something's on the line.
Mazzetti reaches for the fences,
uniform drenched in this good life.
Junkman Turner knows throwing strikes all night
is worth 500 cans clanking empty before noon.
They have been dreaming all winter of this:
the home run trot, the perfect game.
The players chatter the air into frenzy
while the crowd yells its heart out
where they can see it.
They play the game over in the tavern
past midnight until the last song
spins out of the jukebox, snapped up
in the din as they throw themselves out.
To where car doors slam, keys turn
toward home in their ignitions.

All the way back the radio is ecstatic
with the news. He smiles, tugs at his shirt,
the letters of the town heating his chest
the way love used to.

He brakes up the driveway and strikes
a match, a small bargain of light.
He sees his wife's face, quiet
as she leaves the car, moving
without looking back into the house
until he's lost her. His fingers burn
and bring him back to the big game,
another night he's come out on top of.
He's learned the hero's words, to say
how it was nothing when he knows
different, how it must be something
to wind up in the dirt so many times
and sliding, ahead of any throw
or daylight or thought of turning back.
Sliding into home through the dark,
thinking *safe*, in the middle of his life.

WYATT PRUNTY

A Baseball Team of Unknown Navy Pilots, Pacific Theater, 1944

Assigned a week's good bunt, run, throw,
Makeshift uniforms, long practices,
Then games, playoffs, and a round of photos
Stark as this one slipping from its frame,
Where hats, gloves, bats in hand these stood
Lined up and focused, smiling and unnamed—

Till the shutter clicked and each went back,
Retracing zagged geometries
Of the navigator's elbowed tack
And smudged replotted overrule
Pulled from a fix when miles off track
They crabbed the wind and calculated fuel;

And then the wide sleek secret fleet below
Blacked out until the climbing tracers
Sent their bright concussive flak
And going on was all. Time wound,
And some planes banking, others not;
And the one, tail-riddled, easing down,

Crew tossing weight for altitude
Till smoke and someone spelling out a fix.
Then static graveling the words.
And still these faces, whose names we never got,
As all we know is they returned to bases,
Went up when told, came home or not.

Kevin A. González

Ground Rules at Isla Verde Beach

First off: it doesn't matter what inning it is or how many outs
there are, at 4:30 there's a break for half an hour so everyone can run
upstairs & watch *Los Simpsons*, & at five, whoever was on base
goes back to standing on their base, unless there's a decent movie
on Tele-Once, which almost never happens, & whoever was hitting
goes back to the plate, & if it's ten past five & you're still gone,

the game starts without you. If the ball goes past the dunes, it's gone.
If you have two strikes & foul it off into the water, not only are you
    out,
you have to dive & get it. If it goes between the palm trees, it's a hit,
but if it hits a palm tree on the fly, it's a double, & if there's a runner
on first, he's got to hold at third. You should know this: for a movie
to be considered decent it has to be about vicious killer pigs & based

on a true story & have some naked chicks in it. Hey, have you been
    to third base
with a chick yet? Because everybody here has. On Fridays,
    Manny's pop goes
to happy hour & Manny mixes Don Q & Crystal Lite & plays the
    movies
hidden in the sewing kit in the bottom of the closet. Then, he turns
    out
all the lights & throws eggs from the balcony, & downstairs, people
    take off running.
This is what you should know about the guys: If Manny ever hits
    you, hit

him back. If Tito hits you, hit him back. Eric will not hit you. If
    Gadi hits
you, & he will, don't do shit. You've been warned. Don't slide into
    any base
he's covering—he buries glass. He's been known to swipe-tag runners
on the throat. No called strikes, but if he says you're gone, you're gone.
Metal bats are fine, but wood is old school. Here, ball is played
    without
balks or infield fly rules or cups. Okay, this is how you tell if a movie

really sucks: the main guy begins to cry & say, "But this is not a movie!
this is real life!" because motherfucker that's not true, because life
    will hit
you in the balls & no cup will ever save you. Other stuff: if someone
    flies out,
the hit & run is on, but there's no catcher so there's no stolen bases,
& if you're tagging up & the ball beats you to the bag, you have to go
back, even if no one's there to tag you, & whoever has more runs

by nighttime wins, & if it's tied, it ends a tie. If a team goes up by
    ten runs,
it's a KO. Afterwards, you can hit the pool. Then—& this is better
    than a movie—
the Cubs might be on WGN Chicago, & everyone might go
upstairs to watch, & The Hawk or Ryno or Mark Grace might hit
one onto Waveland & take their sweet ass time rounding all the bases,
& always Harry will be singing in the seventh, counting strikes till
    you're out

at the old ball game. What time you out of school? When you get
    home, run
down here & take whichever base is empty. Tonight's a late game,
    no movie
on Tele-Once. Are you ready? You can hit first. Batter up, let's go.

KEVIN MILLER

McNeil Island Penitentiary Closes

The island boat sails
empty one way. For
years I told the kids
of our away games
against fed inmates,
the Native pitcher
with hand-carved knives
tattooed underside
his forearms, his stare
walleyed as search lights
when a kid sixteen
brushed him back. He eyed
me with unwieldy
daggers, safe behind
horizontal bars,
I squatted, signaled
for a curve. Bleacher
bums hooted, howled,
and bet cigarettes
on each pitch. One guy
yelled, He killed seven
guys, watch your back
at the plate. Hitters
joked about playing
the next game at our place.
We split the double
header, and ate lunch
at the big house.

B.H. Fairchild

Body and Soul

Half-numb, guzzling bourbon and Coke from coffee mugs,
our fathers fall in love with their own stories, nuzzling
the facts but mauling the truth, and my friend's father begins
to lay out with the slow ease of a blues ballad a story
about sandlot baseball in Commerce, Oklahoma decades ago.
These were men's teams, grown men, some in their thirties
and forties who worked together in zinc mines or on oil rigs,
sweat and khaki and long beers after work, steel guitar music
whanging in their ears, little white rent houses to return to
where their wives complained about money and broken Kenmores
and then said the hell with it and sang Body and Soul
in the bathtub and later that evening with the kids asleep
lay in bed stroking their husband's wrist tattoo and smoking
Chesterfields from a fresh pack until everything was O.K.
Well, you get the idea. Life goes on, the next day is Sunday,
another ball game, and the other team shows up one man short.

They say, we're one man short, but can we use this boy,
he's only fifteen years old, and at least he'll make a game.
They take a look at the kid, muscular and kind of knowing
the way he holds his glove, with the shoulders loose,
the thick neck, but then with that boy's face under
a clump of angelic blonde hair, and say, oh, hell, sure,
let's play ball. So it all begins, the men loosening up,
joking about the fat catcher's sex life, it's so bad
last night he had to hump his wife, that sort of thing,
pairing off into little games of catch that heat up into

throwing matches, the smack of the fungo bat, lazy jogging
into right field, big smiles and arcs of tobacco juice,
and the talk that gives a cool, easy feeling to the air,
talk among men normally silent, normally brittle and a little
angry with the empty promise of their lives. But they chatter
and say rock and fire, babe, easy out, and go right ahead
and pitch to the boy, but nothing fancy, just hard fastballs
right around the belt, and the kid takes the first two
but on the third pops the bat around so quick and sure
that they pause a moment before turning around to watch
the ball still rising and finally dropping far beyond
the abandoned tractor that marks left field. Holy shit.
They're pretty quiet watching him round the bases,
but then, what the hell, the kid knows how to hit a ball,
so what, let's play some goddamned baseball here.

And so it goes. The next time up, the boy gets a look
at a very nifty low curve, then a slider, and the next one
is the curve again, and he sends it over the Allis Chalmers,
high and big and sweet. The left field just stands there, frozen.
As if this isn't enough, the next time he bats left-handed.
They can't believe it, and the pitcher, a tall, mean-faced
man from Okarche who just doesn't give a shit anyway
because his wife ran off two years ago leaving him with
three little ones and a rusted-out Dodge with a cracked block,
leans in hard, looking at the fat catcher like he was the sonofabitch
who ran off with his wife, leans in and throws something

out of the dark, green hell of forbidden fastballs, something
that comes in at the knees and then leaps viciously towards
the kid's elbow. He swings exactly the way he did right-handed
and they all turn like a chorus line toward deep right field
where the ball loses itself in sagebrush and the sad burnt
dust of dustbowl Oklahoma. It is something to see.

But why make a long story long: runs pile up on both sides,
the boy comes around five times, and five times the pitcher
is cursing both God and His mother as his chew of tobacco sours
into something resembling horse piss, and a ragged and bruised
Spalding baseball disappears into the far horizon. Goodnight,
Irene. They have lost the game and some painful side bets
and they have been suckered. And it means nothing to them
though it should to you when they are told the boy's name is
Mickey Mantle. And that's the story, and those are the facts.
But the facts are not the truth. I think, though, as I scan
the faces of these old men now lost in the innings of their youth,
I think I know what the truth of this story is, and I imagine
it lying there in the weeds behind that Allis Chalmers
just waiting for the obvious question to be asked: why, oh
why in hell didn't they just throw around the kid, walk him,
after he hit the third homer? Anybody would have,
especially nine men with disappointed wives and dirty socks
and diminishing expectations for whom winning at anything
meant everything. Men who knew how to play the game,
who had talent when the other team had nothing except this ringer

who without a pitch to hit was meaningless, and they could go home
with their little two-dollar side bets and stride into the house
singing If You've Got the Money, Honey, I've Got the Time
with a bottle of Southern Comfort under their arms and grab
Dixie or May Ella up and dance across the gray linoleum
as if it were V-Day all over again. But they did not.
And they did not because they were men, and this was a boy.
And they did not because sometimes after making love,
after smoking their Chesterfields in the cool silence and
listening to the big bands on the radio that sounded so glamorous,
so distant, they glanced over at their wives and noticed the lines
growing heavier around the eyes and mouth, felt what their wives
felt: that Les Brown and Glenn Miller and all those dancing couples
and in fact all possibility of human gaiety and light-heartedness
were as far away and unreachable as Times Square or the Avalon
ballroom. They did not because of the gray linoleum lying there
in the half-dark, the free calendar from the local mortuary
that said one day was pretty much like another, the work gloves
looped over the doorknob like dead squirrels. And they did not
because they had gone through a depression and a war that had left
them with the idea that being a man in the eyes of their fathers
and everyone else had cost them just too goddamn much to lay it
at the feet of a fifteen year-old-boy. And so they did not walk him,
and lost, but at least had some ragged remnant of themselves
to take back home. But there is one thing more, though it is not
a fact. When I see my friend's father staring hard into the bottomless
well of home plate as Mantle's fifth homer heads toward Arkansas,
I know that this man with the half-orphaned children and

worthless Dodge has also encountered for the first and possibly
only time the vast gap between talent and genius, has seen
as few have in the harsh light of an Oklahoma Sunday, the blonde
and blue-eyed bringer of truth, who will not easily be forgiven.

IV.

Expanding the Strike Zone

JAMES SCRUTON

Ghost Runners

They haunt the sandlots, load the bases
of memory. On the clearest days
they shimmer over empty infields,

flicker past the chainlink facets
of a backstop, footsteps with the sound
a ball at dusk made through the grass,

whisking quickly into the dark.
They'd score and disappear as needed,
get forced at home and vanish

in the dust they didn't raise, shadow
players, teammates in the mind's eye,
made-up and making up the missing,

coming off a phantom bench to run
all summer. Circling the bases still,
they play absence to its final out.

GAIL MAZUR

Listening to Baseball in the Car

This morning I argued with a friend
about angels. I didn't believe
in his belief in them—I can't
believe they're not a metaphor.
One argument, affectionate,
lacking in animus, went nowhere.
We promised to talk again soon.
Now, when I'm driving away
from Boston and the Red Sox
are losing, I hear the announcer
say, "No angels in the sky today"—
baseball-ese for *a cloudless afternoon*,
no shadows to help a man
who waits in the outfield
staring into the August sun.
Although I know the announcer's
not a rabbi or sage, (no,
he's a sort of sage, disconsolate
philosopher of batting slumps
and injuries), still I scan
the pale blue sky through my
polarized windshield, fervently
hopeful for my fading team
and I feel something a little
foolish, a prayerful throbbing
in my throat and remember
being told years ago that men
are only little lower than

the angels. Floating ahead of me
at the Vermont border, I see
a few wispy horsemane clouds
which I quietly pray will drift
down to Fenway Park where
a demonic opponent has just
slammed another Red Sox pitch,
and the center fielder—call him Jim—
runs back, back, back,
looking heavenward,
and is shielded and doesn't lose
the white ball in the glare.

LINDA GREGERSON

Line Drive Caught by the Grace of God

Half of America doubtless has the whole
of the infield's peculiar heroics by heart,
this one's way with a fractured forearm,
that one with women and off-season brawls,

the ones who are down to business while their owner
goes to the press. You know them already, the quaint
tight pants, the heft
and repose and adroitness of men

who are kept for a while while they age
with the game. It's time
that parses the other fields too,
one time you squander, next time you hoard,

while around the diamond summer runs
its mortal stall, the torso that thickens,
the face that dismantles its uniform.
And sometimes pure felicity, the length

of a player suspended above the dirt
for a wholly deliberate, perfect catch
for nothing, for New York,
for a million-dollar contract which is nothing now,

for free, for the body
as it plays its deft decline and countless humbling,
deadly jokes, so the body
may once have flattered our purposes.

A man like you or me but for this moment's
delay and the grace of God. My neighbor
goes hungry when the Yankees lose,
his wife's too unhappy to cook,

but supper's a small enough price to pay,
he'd tell you himself, for odds
that make the weeks go by so personal,
so hand in glove.

JOE WENDEROTH

Aesthetics of the Bases Loaded Walk

Four times the pitch is outside the strike zone:
high, low, outside, low—four balls.
The man must be given a base, a base on balls.
But there is no base to be given,
no base unoccupied, the bases are full.
Some cannot understand this.
They believe it must be a shameful thing,
lowly forfeit,
the humiliation of man-made rules and chalk boundaries.
They imagine confrontation itself has failed.
Some, even most, don't understand the bases loaded walk,
and they proceed to hiss
or to mock their earlier earnest applause.
But I love it.
They've got no room to put him on.
They put him on. They put him on
and here comes the lowly run
home. Certain, uncontested,
and incomparably calm.
A home-run would have been unbelievable—
the grand slam, loveliest of moments
to glimpse—
but it leads quickly, inevitably, away from us.
Bases empty.
Rally as good as over.
But a walk! a walk! Bases still loaded!
Rally never at a more urgent or capable point!
This is the beauty of it.

The maintenance of a simple danger by way of a good eye.
The inning, the game itself,
hangs in the indelicate balance
of this subtlest method for staying alive,
in the casual implication of unending loss,
in the terrible patience of an anonymous victory.

BRUCE SMITH

Devotion: Baseball

Pinetar, a sluice of tobacco, sunflower seeds and juju.
Lena Blackburne Rubbing Mud, gum, the glues and salves
for doing things fairly—one out of three
swipes at the ball and a flare to right, a dying quail, a 3-
2 change popped up with a *shitfuck*, handcuffed, tomahawked
the high hard stuff or took a backwards K when made to look ugly
as we often were: Humility 3 Arrogance 1 after seven innings. And all
America around us in the sentimental vaudeville. So not the claims
of greened paradise and diamonds and the beauty of the sacrifice
bunt nor the Newtonian symmetries and distances, it was snakes
in the outfield and trances interrupted by a hamstring pull, spit
      and chew,
geological time spans between ball one and ball two. The
      meditative silences
likened to prayer were a bus ride where the Latin music blared.
We had a dominant eye. We had a thought, well, not quite a thought,
a thought fouled off in the direction of a woman who could hold a
      drink,
an oilcan we'd crush like an inside pitch in our dreams. Fast twitch
muscle and jock itch. We scratched our names in dirt.
We wiped our hands on our shirts. As much as we wanted to look
      good,
we were the bullies of our childhood sliding, cleats up at Juan or Bob
with the fury of the psychopath, Ty Cobb (whose mother
blew his father's head off with a shotgun, so forever playing dead).

I liked best the games no one could see: pepper, shagging flies, BP.
Got picked off first and waited for a ticket home.
Drafted or matriculated? In a one-run game I missed the cut-off man.
Boys my age were dying in Khe Sanh.

ELIZABETH POWELL

At the Old Yankee Stadium

The Bronx burned and Ed Koch got his picture taken
With my imaginary husband because he was the bat boy
For the Yankees. We watched baseball most of 1977.
Catfish Hunter threw a ball at everything I didn't like
And tried to smash it. I said: The problem with time is time.
I said this because the imaginary can't always move linearly.
Baseball is never the problem, mostly the solution.
There is no buzzer in baseball.
Everyone you love is everyone you love in 1977
Because we hadn't invented ironic distance yet.
My imaginary husband was on the plane with Thurman Munson,
Like baseball he was beyond death. 7-7-77
We got hitched in the dugout, Billy Martin officiating,
Taking the cross from his cap, making us both
Kiss it. My imaginary husband was Catholic,
I wasn't. The heat kept climbing and I was scared;
The minutes congealed into the footage
Of the game before it looked old.
We had our imaginary baby the next miracle
October, named him Reggie for the homeruns.
But first the lights went out and the trouble
Started with the real, and my imaginary husband stayed
Out late ransacking the streets. While things burned
The rain stopped working, so that
No one knew what was what anymore.
My mother became a man and didn't understand
My imaginary husband. *No such thing*
As gender, she said. *No such thing as real*, quoth I.

Melissa Ludtke's in the locker room, (s)he said.
And girls can join Little League now, you know.
My mood ring was purple most of the time, which meant
I was becoming more visible with a kind of looting intensity,
Like the great silence of my imaginary husband
Rounding the bases, sliding so fast into home
He made the present emerge right here,
The old stadium gone.

ROBERT PACK

The Fan's Soliloquy

Were we not put on earth to play,
To strive to win and be the best?
I might have stayed at home all day
And mowed the lawn, been useful, but
I would have missed the game in which
Broad summer is made manifest.
For restless aging fans like me,
Battle's a laughing metaphor,
With tactics of the stolen base,
A covert strategy like war—
The fight to win the pennant race.
The 9th—and all seems lost, but then
We fool them with a bunt—a chance
If missed that will not come again—
To make the eager troops advance
Unless the runner's tagged at home,
The opportunity to score
Is lost, like the lost souls of men,
Now merely shades, for whom no more
Will winning laughter come again.
And so confronted with the fate
Defeat tells us that we deserve
As when a batter hugs the plate,
Misses for the decreed three times
And wonders if that pitcher's curve
Could sneak down past a rooster's glare,
A slugger doomed to whiff the air,
Or water organized into a fountain

Overflowing with itself.
An arrowhead can now be used
As an adornment for a necklace
Like a flower in a painting where a stream
Leaps past a light-reflecting rock
With nothing in a brushstroke left to accident.
     And so our accidental meeting on the rock
Flowed by, a flower cast upon the water
With intent unknown, and all
That's left now is the arrowhead.

LOU LIPSITZ

Why Baseball Doesn't Matter

It's not because the game's so slow,
that the pitcher has to step down off the mound,
pick up the resin bag, adjust his hat, adjust
his pants, spit, pound his glove,
step back onto the rubber,
then peer down, get the sign
nod approval and only then rear back,
and unleash the baseball.

It's not that basketball has more action:
the gliding down court—dragonflies in a mating dance.
Start then stop, backtrack, fake,
then dart toward the basket.

Nor that football has that heavy military vibe,
with the tanks moving into position,
the "bomb" lofted downfield, and the
grim drama of the goal line stand
some beachhead, Iwo Jima,
young men pinned down in the mud.

And it's not that America's altogether
changed (though it has). It's not
the steroid home runs, not
those million dollar player salaries,
not the glitzy gold chains

around their expensive necks,
not the greedy owners, not that the Dodgers
left Brooklyn and the Braves left Boston or
the . . . what was it . . . left where?

It's that tonight, in midsummer,
under an inquisitive fraction of a moon,
the wind pulls a thin blanket of dust
off the distant fields and carries it for miles.

I feel the black edges of night
like a curled fern leaf about to unfold,
and a small grasshopper
settles on my hand and I lift it and
watch it, suddenly, fly from me
like a knuckle ball, like the startling,
crooked spirit of grief.

And I stand up and look around
and find myself alone
for the long seventh inning stretch,
tiny night lights appearing inevitably
over this mysterious, damaged world
of triumphs.

KEVIN STEIN

Baseball Arrives in Richmond, Indiana

As if winter bore remorse for its game
of hide and seek, I bend down among
the wild iris and purple dame's rocket,
shucking leaves foolish enough to trust
April's disarming come-hither blush.
Winter's parting kiss, my Angela calls it,
as dangerous as all love must be,
why else the budding and blossom and decay?
Which is to say it's noon, I'm drunk,
and none of this has anything to do
with flowers. All morning I drank
with guests, men who fed an arm or leg
to the great beast of the Republic
so hungry for peace it ate itself alive.
These, I found beside in swamp or woods
or tattered field. These, war spit back,
partial and aggrieved. They were not
as lucky as I, nor as lucky as the dead.
I know it's simple chance that saved me—
not courage or prayer or anything
I might claim as my own. Still I've guilt
enough to keep my distance from the park,
though cheers lift like grackles flapping
through molasses sky: slow to rise,
quick to fall. Always I turn too late
to see what's caused such glee, always
my eye catches the blue clump of amputees
who lean on crutches or hang an empty sleeve,

unable to clap or stand at ease. Four years
after the Great War, I watch our Quaker City
club "do honest battle," as the newspaper says,
with lordly Knightstown. And win.
A peaceful lot, those Quaker men had nothing
of Lincoln's war. They prayed instead,
and God forgive them, kept their hardy limbs.

MARJORIE MADDOX

Grand Slam

Dreams brimming over,
childhood stretched out in legs,
this is the moment replayed on winter days
when frost covers the field,
when age steals away wishes.
Glorious sleep that seeps back there
to the glory of our baseball days.

GAIL MAZUR

Baseball

For John Limon

The game of baseball is not a metaphor
and I know it's not really life.
The chalky green diamond, the lovely
dusty brown lanes I see from airplanes
multiplying around the cities
are only neat playing fields.
Their structure is not the frame
of history carved out of forest,
that is not what I see on my ascent.

And down in the stadium,
the veteran catcher guiding the young
pitcher through the innings, the line
of concentration between them,
that delicate filament is not
like the way you are helping me,
only it reminds me when I strain
for analogies, the way a rookie strains
for perfection, and the veteran,
in his wisdom, seems to promise it,
it glows from his upheld glove,

and the man in front of me
in the grandstand, drinking banana
daiquiris from a thermos,
continuing through a whole dinner

to the aromatic cigar even as our team
is shut out, nearly hitless, he is
not like the farmer that Auden speaks
of in Breughel's Icarus,
or the four inevitable woman-hating
drunkards, yelling, hugging
each other and moving up and down
continuously for more beer

and the young wife trying to understand
what a full count could be
to please her husband happy in
his old dreams, or the little boy
in the Yankees cap already nodding
off to sleep against his father,
program and popcorn memories
sliding into the future,
and the old woman from Lincoln, Maine,
screaming at the Yankee slugger
with wounded knees to break his leg
this is not a microcosm,
not even a slice of life

and the terrible slumps,
when the greatest hitter mysteriously
goes hitless for weeks, or
the pitcher's stuff is all junk
who threw like a magician all last month,

or the days when our guys look
like Sennett cops, slipping, bumping
each other, then suddenly, the play
that wasn't humanly possible, the Kid
we know isn't ready for the big leagues,
leaps into the air to catch a ball
that should have gone downtown,
and coming off the field is hugged
and bottom-slapped by the sudden
sorcerers, the winning team
the question of what makes a man
slump when his form, his eye,
his power aren't to blame, this isn't
like the bad luck that hounds us,
and his frustration in the games
not like our deep rage
for disappointing ourselves

the ball park is an artifact,
manicured, safe, "scene in an Easter egg,"
and the order of the ball game,
the firm structure with the mystery
of accidents always contained,
not the wild field we wander in,
where I'm trying to recite the rules,
to repeat the statistics of the game,
and the wind keeps carrying my words away.

V.

Screwballs and Double Plays

WYATT PRUNTY

Baseball

About the time I got my first-baseman's mitt
I heard that Dizzy Dean was sacked
Because he made a dirty comment
Over the air. Camera zoomed and locked
On a young couple kissing, something slipped
With Dizzy, who then made the call:
"He kisses her on every strike,
And she kisses him on the balls."

In a century banked with guilt and doubt
Sometimes the telling moments come
As inadvertently as Dizzy's joke,
Like Hitler's code before Coventry was bombed,
Or Valery's remark about Descartes,
"I sometimes think, therefore I sometimes am."

LISA OLSTEIN

Dream in Which I Love a Third Baseman

At first he seemed a child,
dirt on his lip and the sun
lighting up his hair behind him.

All around us, the hesitation
of year-rounders who know
the warmer air will bring crowds.

No one goes to their therapist
to talk about how happy they are,
but soon I'd be back in the dugout

telling my batting coach how
the view outside my igloo seemed
to be changing, as if the night

sky were all the light there is.
Now, like two babies reaching
through the watery air to touch soft

fingers to soft forehead, like blind fish
sensing a familiar fluttering in the waves,
slowly, by instinct, we became aware.

Off-field, outside the park, beyond
the gates, something was burning.
The smell was everywhere.

Tossing the Bouquet

In the ninth, Mariano shreds
another bat that leaves a lazy can
of corn dropping in left field
while something resembling
a bouquet of wooden shards
falls between first and home.
When my sister threw hers,
she aimed right for me but
in her drunken exuberance
it veered off like a wild pitch.
And I, the player trying to
"do too much," twisted into
the batter's box and nearly
broke my knees trying to hold
up my swing to avoid the strike.
Another bridesmaid caught
her bouquet that I'd held
in the church in an easy basket
catch, then looked triumphant
as a stranger ran the garter under
her silk gown and over her thigh.

Aaron Belz

Second Base

Sometimes when someone says something crazy
I tell them they're out in left field.
The only people you can't say this to are
actual left fielders. People like Barry Bonds.
If Barry Bonds says something that has
nothing to do with the subject at hand
and you tell him he's out in left field,
he's going to think he's doing his job.
He's going to think he gets paid
to make comments like that, but he's wrong.
Similarly, yet also slightly differently,
when Barry Bonds fails to follow through,
doesn't return a call, misses an appointment,
and you say, man, you really dropped the ball,
he'll take it seriously—maybe for the wrong reason,
but at least he'll try to do better next time.
One time I left a voicemail for Barry Bonds
and said it was urgent he call me right away,
and he didn't return my call for two weeks,
and when he did, he said something
that had nothing to do with the voicemail I'd left.
I didn't know what to say that wouldn't confuse him.
To compound things, it was the third time
he had screwed up like this. He was out.
As he walked slowly back to the bench,
dramatically unbuckling his elbow armor,
I thought I heard him muttering something

and warned him that he'd better just sit down.
When Jeff Kent came to bat, I joked
that I'd gotten to second base with Barry Bonds.
He didn't see anything unusual about that.

PAMELA YENSER

Summer Games

Blame me.
Blame
history.
Or blame
yourself if
life lies
foul and
love's a
mystery
(foul play!)
we half
realize
through our
fingers in
the dark—
like those
leather-hard,
hand-sewn
balls of
flesh which
symbolize
your sex.
To each his
own.

Now give
me your
hand—and

glove.
Let me
show you a
softer
mound,
greener
fields empty
with love,
a lighter
stick to
swing
around.
You started
this game in
the first
place,
bragging
how you'd
gotten to
first base.

BOB HICOK

Root root root for the home team

They spit too much in baseball, I can't watch,
I don't like spitting, we should be elegant,
sling garbage in suits, not throw balls
at each other's heads and spit, not slide
spikes high and spit, are these men drowning?,
what's the rule when you need both a question mark
and a comma after a sentence?, should I spit now
that I've asked?, are you spitting on your way out
to pick the kids up from skating?, my allegiance
is to the grass, spit on in front of sixty-thousand people,
such a beautiful translation of sun, everything I want
from plant life, to be the bed of summer sleep,
to be soft in catching my stumbles, labor is weak,
on the defensive, I say we lead grass in a strike,
No More Spitting on some of the signs we'll carry,
High and Dry also drives the point home, look, a pun,
but you don't see me spitting now, do you?, or after metaphors
spitting, God help us if poets spit after alliterating,
I never tried that word as a verb, give it a shot,
it's like a line drive in your mouth, let's celebrate,
I've got sparklers, we can burn things, we'll keep our fluids
to ourselves, this is what civilized people do, and art,
they do that too, make walls and then make walls prettier,
I bet Picasso was a big spitter, you had to watch
where you stepped during his blue period, Van Gogh
never spit, not ever once in this life, but if he did
it would have been in a lively, shimmery, I-am-going-mad
sort of way, there he is, stretching a single into a double,

looking at the second baseman's head, noticing how it moves,
how the colors are breakers of light, the score
is Yankees twelve, Painters yellow, what could be more American
than the stolen base?

ANDREW HUDGINS

In the Red Seats

High in the red seats'
vertiginous, steep,
narrow rows, I stood
to let four drunks edge by,
and one, back turned to the field,
side-shuffled down the row,
shouting, "Hi! Great game!"
into averted faces.
Great game? It was nothing—
nothing in the first inning.
He breathed beer in my face. Our eyes
met and the force of meeting
seemed to tip him backward. He teetered,
flailed. I reached out, grabbed
his shoulder, pulled him erect
and past erect till we
were leaning forehead to forehead,
touching, and his eyes
flooded with love. He tossed
both arms around me, sobbed,
"You saved my life, man.
I swear I'll never forget you."
"Yeah, sure you will," I said
and slapped his back,
a quick, bluff way of saying,
"You're ok, pal" and "Hey,
let go." He nodded, shuffled
to his seat with his drunk buddies,

and one, as he slid past,
bobbed his eyebrows at me
and shrugged.
                    Five seats away,
from an adoring, pink,
intoxicated face,
love shimmered, love radiated
like equatorial sunshine,
the way a lover's face
illuminates the lover,
the loved, and the dark world
in one strange, lucent moment:
satisfied and thrilled, intense
and effortless—as God
regards us every moment.
I couldn't bear it. I left
in the fifth inning, sidling
down packed precipitous
red rows, easing past strangers,
excusing myself.

VI.

At the Letters

TOM CLARK

Baseball & Classicism

Every day I peruse the box scores for hours
Sometimes I wonder why I do it
Since I am not going to take a test on it
And no one is going to give me money

The pleasure's something like that of codes
Of deciphering an ancient alphabet say
So as brightly to picturize Eurydice
In the Elysian Fields on her perfect day

The day she went 5 for 5 against Vic Raschi

George Bowering

Opening Day

For George Stanley

On opening day
        you can open your stance,
        you can open a book,

take a good look, yeah,
        take a liking, like
        to a Viking.

Take a swing at a thing
        like a sinker, ahuh,
        be a thinker,

think of getting down to second,
        take a second.
        take a look.
        take a lead-off,
        read a book.

Rounding third, like a bird,
        read the sign
        from your coach,
        your approach

to the plate,
isn't late,
isn't great,
but okay, okay, okay,

okay, you're safe,
safe at home,
read a poem,
read *this* poem,

read about base,
read about ball,
read about baseball.

I mean don't delay it.
Get down and play it.

MARIANNE MOORE

Baseball and Writing

Suggested by post-game broadcasts

Fanaticism? No. Writing is exciting
and baseball is like writing.
    You can never tell with either
        how it will go
        or what you will do;
    generating excitement—
    a fever in the victim—
    pitcher, catcher, fielder, batter.
            Victim in what category?
*Owl*man watching from the press box?
        To whom does it apply?
        Who is excited? Might it be I?

It's a pitcher's battle all the way—a duel—
a catcher's, as, with cruel
    puma paw, Elston Howard lumbers lightly
        back to plate. (His spring
        de-winged a bat swing.)
    They have that killer instinct;
    yet Elston—whose catching
    arm has hurt them all with the bat—
        when questioned, says, unenviously,
"I'm very satisfied. We won."
        Shorn of the batting crown, says, "We";
        robbed by a technicality.

When three players on a side play three positions
and modify conditions,
    the massive run need not be everything.
        "Going, going . . . " Is
        it? Roger Maris
    has it, running fast. You will
    never see a finer catch. Well . . .
    "Mickey, leaping like the devil"—why
            gild it, although deer sounds better—
snares what was speeding towards its treetop nest,
            one-handing the souvenir-to-be
            meant to be caught by you or me.

Assign Yogi Berra to Cape Canaveral;
he could handle any missile.
    He is no feather. "Strike! . . . Strike *two!*"
        Fouled back. A blur.
        It's gone. You would infer
    that the bat had eyes.
    He put the wood to that one.
Praised, Skowron says, "Thanks, Mel.
    I think I helped a *little* bit."
            All business, each, and modesty.
        Blanchard, Richardson, Kubek, Boyer.
            In that galaxy of nine, say which
            won the pennant? *Each.* It was he.

Those two magnificent saves from the knee—throws
by Boyer, finesses in twos—
    like Whitey's three kinds of pitch and pre-
        diagnosis
        with pick-off psychosis.
    Pitching is a large subject.
    Your arm, too true at first, can learn to
    catch your corners—even trouble
        Mickey Mantle. ("Grazed a Yankee!
My baby pitcher, Montejo!"
        With some pedagogy,
        you'll be tough, premature prodigy.)

They crowd him and curve him and aim for the knees. Trying
indeed! The secret implying:
    "I can stand here, bat held steady."
    One may suit him;
    none has hit him.
    Imponderables smite him.
    Muscle kinks, infections, spike wounds
    require food, rest, respite from ruffians. (Drat it!
        Celebrity costs privacy!)
Cow's milk, "tiger's milk," soy milk, carrot juice,
        brewer's yeast (high potency—
        concentrates presage victory

sped by Luis Arroyo, Hector Lopez—
deadly in a pinch. And "Yes,
    it's work; I want you to bear down,
        but enjoy it
        while you're doing it."
    Mr. Houk and Mr. Sain,
    if you have a rummage sale,
    don't sell Roland Sheldon or Tom Tresh.
        Studded with stars in belt and crown,
the Stadium is an adastrium.
        O flashing Orion,
        your stars are muscled like the lion.

Franklin Pierce Adams

A Ballad of Baseball Burdens

The burden of hard hitting. Slug away
  Like Honus Wagner or like Tyrus Cobb.
Else fandom shouteth: "Who said you could play?
  Back to the jasper league, you minor slob!"
  Swat, hit, connect, line out, get on the job.
Else you shall feel the brunt of fandom's ire
  Biff, bang it, clout it, hit it on the knob—
This is the end of every fan's desire.

The burden of good pitching. Curved or straight.
  Or in or out, or haply up or down,
To puzzle him that standeth by the plate,
  To lessen, so to speak, his bat-renoun:
  Like Christy Mathewson or Miner Brown,
So pitch that every man can but admire
  And offer you the freedom of the town—
This is the end of every fan's desire.

The burden of loud cheering. O the sounds!
  The tumult and the shouting from the throats
Of forty thousand at the Polo Grounds
  Sitting, ay, standing *sans* their hats and coats.
  A mighty cheer that possibly denotes
That Cub or Pirate fat is in the fire;
  Or, as H. James would say, We've got their goats—
This is the end of every fan's desire.

The burden of a pennant. O the hope,
        The tenuous hope, that hope that's half a fear,
The lengthy season and the boundless dope,
        And the bromidic; "Wait until next year."
        O dread disgrace of trailing in the rear,
O Piece of Bunting, flying high and higher
        That next October it shall flutter here:
This is the end of every fan's desire.

ENVOY

Ah, Fans, let not the Quarry but the Chase
        Be that to which most fondly we aspire!
For us not Stake, but Game; not Goal, but Race—
        THIS is the end of every fan's desire.

FLOYD SKLOOT

Whitman Pinch Hits, 1861

After six months of the wandering Whitman found himself
at the edge of a Long Island potato farm in early fall.
He saw a squad of young men at sport on sparse grass.
Looking up, he saw a few stray geese rise and circle back
north as though confused by the sudden Indian summer,
then looked down to study cart tracks cut deep into the mud.
Weary of his own company, shorn of appetite, he thought
it would be sweet to sit awhile beside this field and watch
the boys in their shabby flannel uniforms playing ball.
Caught between wanting to look at them and wanting
them to look at him, he could not tell from this distance
if the torn and faded blues they wore were soldiers' clothes
or baseball clothes. But he loved the rakish tilt of their caps
and cocky chatter drifting on the mid-day air. He had seen
the game played before, in Brooklyn, on a pebbled patch
laid out beside the sea, and thought it something young,
something brotherly for the frisky young and their brothers
to do in the shadow of civil war. That seemed two lifetimes
ago, not two years. The face he could no longer bear to find
in a mirror looked now like this island's ploughed ground.
Time does turn thick, Whitman thought, does press itself
against a man's body as he moves through a world torn apart
by artillery fire and weeping. Without knowing it happened,

he settled on a rise behind the makeshift home, moving
as he moved all year, a ghost in his own life. He should write
about baseball for the *Eagle*, or better still, make an epic poem
of it. The diamond chalked on grass, stillness held in a steady

light before the burst of movement, boys with their faces open
to the sky as a struck ball rose toward the all-consuming clouds.
But it was the sound that held him rapt. Wild, musical voices
punctuated by a pock of bat on ball, then the dropped wood
clattering to earth, grunts, everyone in motion through the air,
the resistant air, and then the lovely laughter. Whitman laughed
with them, a soundless gargle. The next batter staggered and fell,
drunk, his chin tobacco-splattered, laughing at his own antics
as he limped back to the felled tree where teammates sat.
They shook their heads, ignoring the turned ankle he exposed
for them to admire. Suddenly all eyes turned toward Whitman
where he lounged, propped on one elbow, straw hat tilted
to keep the sun from his neck, on the hill that let him see
everything at once. They beckoned. They needed Whitman
to pinch hit, to keep the game going into its final inning.
The injured batter held his stick out, thick end gripped in his fist,
and barked a curse. Whitman sat up, the watcher summoned
into a scene he has forgotten he did not create. They beckoned
and he came toward them like a bather moving through
thigh-high breakers, time stopping and then turning back,
letting him loose at last amid the spirits that greeted him
as the boys pounded his back, as they turned him around
and shoved him toward the field. In his hands, the wood
felt light. He stood beside the folded coat that represented
home, shifted his weight and stared at the pitcher who glared
back, squinting against the sun, taking the poet's measure.

Amy Newman

from While Sylvia Plath Studies *The Joy of Cooking* on Her Honeymoon in Benidorm, Spain, Delmore Schwartz Reclines in the Front Seat of His Buick Roadmaster

While Sylvia Plath studies *The Joy of Cooking* on her honeymoon
in Benidorm, Spain,
Delmore Schwartz reclines in the front seat of his Buick
Roadmaster
listening to a Giants game on the car radio.
The car's parked on his farmland in Baptistown,
New Jersey, where obstinate plants attempt survival
at great odds, their vital spikes insulting and defending.
The thistle fans its prickly leaves,
the burdock hustles, miserly. Its dry-as-death seed
will outlast you, traveler, its dry-as-hope seedling will use you,
tenacious as the leftover god, the eye-of-the-needle god,
the straggly one, the Shylock, who lent you your life,
who chose this desert wilderness for exile.
He manifests the empty field for you to wander.
He removeth your brilliance and set you in a basket
alone among the rushes. He maketh the coral of Seconal
and suffers you to recline in the evergreen Dexamyl shade,
while Ernie Harwell calls the last out
(Willie Jones popping up to Al Dark)
in the car's radium glow. Do you see it, American poetry?
The happy arc of the ball above Shibe Park—
a moment of promise falling off, coming to nothing.
Disappearing to atoms. Giants win, 4-2.

MARVIN BELL

In America

these things happen: I am taken
to see a friend
who talks too fast and is now teaching Moby Dick
according to jujitsu,
or judo according to Melville:
He says Melville gets you leaning
and lets go, or gets you to pulling
and suddenly advances, retreats
when you respond, and so on. Ok, I
accept that, but then he starts
in on the assassination of
John F. Kennedy as planned by our
government, and he has a collection of
strange deaths at handy times
bizarrely of people who know something.
I know nothing. I want to know
nothing whatsoever. It once
was enough to be standing
on a field of American baseball,
minding my ground balls and business,
when the infielder to my left
shot me the news of what is now known as
The Bay of Pigs, then in progress
but secretly, and certainly
doomed for stupidity, mis-timing,
marsh-landings, and JFK's resolve
to unaccomplish the Agency's fait accompli
by refusing air cover. This would crackle

the air waves, but later. Tall tales,
I figured, wrongly,
putting my fist in my glove
for America.
Moby Dick, you damn whale,
I've seen whales.
America, though—
too big to be seen.

DAVE MCGIMPSEY

from The History of Baseball

Henry Wadsworth Longfellow

Let's be clear. I'm going to towel-snap you
out the way. Don't act like you don't know.
Please don't pretend you don't have it coming.
You may be late for your game of Blue Jays.

Baseball is great without your poetry.
Particularly when your last poems
spoke of "grief, anger, madness and death"
but said nothing about Dr. Pepper.

I'm not getting better. I can make fun
of how my doctor looks like Lurch all I want,
it doesn't light lanterns in the Old North Church
or make me think your face isn't stupid.

If I was to start praying, it would not be
for my life. It would be that the Yankees
win yet another World Series Championship.
It's an insult to pray for the impossible.

Ralph Waldo Emerson

If Ronald Reagan never existed,
Emerson would invent him. "Here's a man,"
he'd write, "who will invent swimming pools
and will jackknife into bald eagle soup."

Emerson, however, would hate baseball,
particularly if he had the sense
there would be a franchise in Atlanta
and Larry Jones's nickname would be "Chipper."

The truth is, actually, nothing denies
the authority of an intellectual life
like the body: big hit, nice waist, strong arm,
pretty hair, fat man falls on the Queen.

Emerson's immunity to the condition
that would be known in literary circles
as "Looking Toronto" is worth noting.
Nobody needs to know what a bunt is.

F. Scott Fitzgerald

Gatsby studied the manners of baseball
to "fit in." The best way to fit in baseball
is to go to the track in Saratoga,
and—*Kobayashi Maru*—fix the World Series.

I grew up anglophone in French Quebec.
The neighbors looked at me and said *"vers l'enfers,
mon ennemi héréditaire !"* which means
"My dear friend, you're welcome to live in peace."

My mother made me a steak for my first
Little League game, which might as well have been
Excelsiors versus Knickerbockers
in some sunlit Manhattan cricket patch.

I think the best way to fit into Quebec
is to not think it that different from Cleveland,
at least that seemed plausible with the Expos,
then, you cope as others do—with alcohol.

Saul Bellow

Nobody cruising to thirty home runs,
a hundred RBIs is thinking
"I hope my creative writing professor
likes my poem about writing poems."

Saul Bellow's Moses Herzog's "fuckyknuckles"
were the excuse for why he, man enough,
still wasn't cut for baseball. Fair enough.
Nobody leaves baseball for literature.

Delmore Schwartz, the real-life Humboldt Fleisher
in Saul Bellow's roman-à-clef *Humboldt's Gift*,
despairingly wondered why poetry
couldn't excite him the way the Giants did.

It hurts he couldn't consider how the Giants
were having a better season than poetry,
and one day, MFA programs would admit
all the fuckyknucklers they could handle.

ROBERT PINSKY

The City

I live in the little village of the present
But lately I forget my neighbors' names.
More and more I spend my days in the City:

The great metropolis where I can hope
To glimpse great spirits as they cross the street
Souls durable as the cockroach and the lungfish.

When I was young, I lived in a different village.
We had parades: the circus, the nearby fort.
And Rabbi Gewirtz invented a game called "Baseball."

To reach first base you had to chant two lines
Of Hebrew verse correctly. Mistakes were outs.
One strike for every stammer or hesitation.

We boys were thankful for the Rabbi's grace,
His balancing the immensity of words
Written in letters of flame by God himself

With our mere baseball, the little things we knew...
Or do I remember wrong, did we boys think
(There were no girls) that baseball was the City

And that the language we were learning by rote—
A little attention to meaning, now and then—
Was small and local. The Major Leagues, the City.

BARRY SPACKS

The Catch

In memory of James Wright

His words make the heart shiver
as when dawn
invades the darkness, or dusk
the light.

He could sense, in a turtle
—neck-stretched, hopeful—
all the sadness
and hunger of life.

Say he was out there
seeing it
a long time coming,
his going . . .

his insouciance
beautiful to watch—
easy glance over shoulder
moving toward the wall,

toward the miraculous
catch
in the pounded leather glove
in far left field.

SARAH GRIDLEY

The Minors

Evening posing in the glamour getup of field lights, into dry valley
      ash echoes over mown grass, over painted
diamond, hypnagogic. By this green distinction done
      & undone all
inhale, all murmur & applause plowed deep
      down & numerous
in the air. At the plate below
      the heavens' sickle,
heart weaves to unravel its red
      bolts in patience. The boys are setting out
and coming home:
      Ulysses & Ulysses & Ulysses

VII.

Greats of the Game

Rolfe Humphries

Polo Grounds

Time is of the essence. This is a highly skilled
And beautiful mystery. Three or four seconds only
From the time that Riggs connects till he reaches first,
And in those seconds Jurges goes to his right,
Comes up with the ball, tosses to Witek at second,
For the force on Reese, Witek to Mize at first,
In time for the out—a double play.

(Red Barber crescendo. Crowd noises, obligatio;
Scattered staccatos from the peanut boys,
Loud in the lull, as the teams are changing sides)...

Hubbell takes the sign, nods, pumps, delivers—
A foul into the stands. Dunn takes a new ball out,
Hands it to Danning, who throws it down to Werber;
Werber takes off his glove, rubs the ball briefly,
Tosses it over to Hub, who goes to the rosin bag,
Takes the sign from Danning, pumps, delivers—
Low outside, ball three. Danning goes to the mound,
Says something to Hub, Dunn brushes off the plate,
Adams starts throwing in the Giant bullpen,
Hub takes the sign from Danning, pumps, delivers,
Camilli gets hold of it, a long fly to the outfield,
Ott goes back, back, back, against the wall, gets under it,
Pounds his glove, and takes it for the out.
That's all for the Dodgers....
Time is of the essence. The rhythms break,
More varied and subtle than any kind of dance;

Movement speeds up or lags. The ball goes out
In sharp and angular drives, or long slow arcs,
Comes in again controlled and under aim;
The players wheel or spurt, race, stoop, slide, halt,
Shift imperceptibly to new positions,
Watching the signs according to the batter,
The score, the inning. Time is of the essence.

Time is of the essence. Remember Terry?

Remember Stonewall Jackson, Lindstrom, Frisch,

When they were good? Remember Long George Kelly?

Remember John McGraw and Benny Kauff?
Remember Bridwell, Tenney, Merkle, Youngs,
Chief Meyers, Big Jeff Tesreau, Shufflin' Phil?
Remember Mathewson, Ames, and Donlin,
Buck Ewing, Rusie, Smiling Mickey Welch?

Remember a left-handed catcher named Jack Humphries,
Who sometimes played the outfield, in '83?

Time is of the essence. The shadow moves
From the plate to the box, from the box to second base,
From second to the outfield, to the bleachers.

Time is of the essence. The crowd and players
Are the same age always, but the man in the crowd
Is older every season. Come on, play ball!

CHARLES HARPER WEBB

Shadow Ball

Let's say some black guys in the '30s hustled up a baseball game;
then right away this tree-trunk-armed Josh Gibson type
lambasted their one soggy Spalding-with-its-cover-falling-off
over the sarsparillas into Okeefokee Slough. Next play,
the pitcher wound up, and threw a fat nothing. The batter
swung, and smoked a low line drive the shortstop blocked,
and fired to the first baseman, who did a split and scooped
nothing out of the dirt just as the runner banged the bag.
"Out!" roared the umpire, and both benches cleared.

The Pittsburgh Crawfords, Birmingham Black Barons,
New York Black Yankees, even the Indianapolis Clowns
beat the best white teams at real baseball. Still, before
a game, they'd whip around-the-horn that spherical hunk
of the void they knew so well—slamming it deep, chasing it
down so skillfully few whites who saw them guessed the trick.
Black folks were shadows to most white ones anyway,
though it was whites who pioneered the shadow services
for which government is famed, and the shadow intelligence

displayed inside high offices across the land,
not to mention shadow marriage, where couples
make real mortgage payments to shadow companies
for shadow homes, have shadow sex, and before they sleep
with shadow partners, say "I love you" without

the shadowiest notion what they mean, which is why
their kids prefer the well-lit screens of movies and the world-
wide web to baseball, and professional theorists swear
there's no *real* life, *real* meaning, *real* excellence, real *real*,

and the most enlightened answer to "Good Night" is *"Good*
is a race/class/gender-determined abstraction. And it's not night.
The sky just looks that way." Yes, it looks darker every day.
Those Negro League All-Stars—Oscar Charleston, Willie Wells,
Buck Leonard, Cool Papa Bell—who couldn't stay
in white hotels, but who apparently enjoyed life anyway,
can be forgiven if they laugh in their all-black graveyards
to see shadows reach out black gloves and grab us all.

NICHOLAS RIPATRAZONE

Box Joseph

5 foot 5. 202. Triceps like flanks. Dockworker. Walked out of school after the first grade. Catcher. Threw from the crouch. Pants tight at the quads. Scrambled eggs for lunch and dinner. Slept in his uniform before games on the road. Smoked High Admirals and dipped Copenhagen. Drank brandy with milk, the mix a thin brown. Knocked an in-the-park home run the night Babe Ruth hit his first. Had a son. Said it was with one woman and then with another. His mother sat him down with the pastor and they made a list. Anna, Teresa, Gwendolyn, Sarah, Terri. Definitely not Terri, he said, and leaned back. They decided on Anna and he went to her house with roses and pound cake. Her boyfriend opened the door and stood face to face with Box, with that strength of knowing that he stood in his own home. Box set the roses and cake on the front porch and left. A week later Anna left the boy on Box's front porch. His mother watched the boy and named him Jude. She chose the name. Eyes some days blue and others green. She changed his clothes on a washboard. Mashed peaches with a fork and drained the juice. Box stuffed gauze in his mitt. Constant back problems. Took baths with primrose, sweet violet, and willow bark. Slept on a bare bed, slept on springs. One game he fell forward onto home plate in the midst of a batter's swing. The bat missed his head by the width of a leaf. Walked the rest of his life with a cane. When his mother died he took the boy back home. He was only 6. The boy brought him walking sticks from the woods. Pine and oak. Pared them down with a knife, smoothed them with sandpaper. Held his father's hand as they walked down the street. The boy picked up a bat when he was 8. It felt good in his hands. Box said his swing was crisp. There really is nothing like that snap.

QUINCY TROUPE

Poem for My Father

For Quincy T. Trouppe, Sr.

father, it was an honor to be there, in the dugout
with you, the glory of great black men swinging their lives
at bats, at tiny white balls
burning in at unbelievable speeds, riding up & in & out
a curve breaking down wicked, like a ball falling off a table
moving away, snaking down, screwing its stitched magic
into chitlin circuit air, its comma seams spinning
toward breakdown, dipping, like a hipster
bebopping a knee-dip stride, in the charlie parker forties
wrist curling, like a swan's neck
behind a slick black back
cupping an invisible ball of dreams

& you there, father, regal, as an african, obeah man
sculpted out of wood, from a sacred tree, of no name, no place, origin
thick branches branching down, into cherokee & someplace else lost
way back in africa, the sap running dry
crossing from north carolina into georgia, inside grandmother mary's
womb, where your mother had you in the violence of that red soil
ink blotter news, gone now, into blood graves
of american blues, sponging rococo
truth long gone as dinosaurs
the agent-oranged landscape of former names
absent of african polysyllables, dry husk, consonants there
now, in their place, names, flat, as polluted rivers
& that guitar string smile always snaking across

some virulent, american, redneck's face
scorching, like atomic heat, mushrooming over nagasaki
& hiroshima, the fever blistered shadows of it all
inked, as etchings, into sizzled concrete
but you, there, father, through it all, a yardbird solo
riffing on bat & ball glory, breaking down the fabricated myths
of white major league legends, of who was better than who
beating them at their own crap
game, with killer bats, as bud powell swung his silence into beauty
of a josh gibson home run, skittering across piano keys of bleachers
shattering all manufactured legends up there in lights
struck out white knights, on the risky edge of amazement
awe, the miraculous truth sluicing through
steeped & disguised in the blues
confluencing, like the point at the cross
when a fastball hides itself up in a slider, curve
breaking down & away in a wicked, sly grin
curved & posed as an ass-scratching uncle tom, who
like old satchel paige delivering his famed hesitation pitch
before coming back with a hard, high, fast one, is slicker
sliding, & quicker than a professional hitman—
the deadliness of it all, the sudden strike
like that of the "brown bomber's" crossing right
of sugar ray robinson's, lightning, cobra bite

& you, there, father, through it all, catching rhythms
of chono pozo balls, drumming, like conga beats into your
    catcher's mitt

hard & fast as "cool papa" bell jumping into bed
before the lights went out

of the old, negro baseball league, a promise, you were
father, a harbinger, of shock waves, soon come

BRIAN TURNER

Jackie

For Virne Beatrice "Jackie" Mitchell, pitcher (1912–1987)

It doesn't matter if you wore a fake beard
barnstorming with a club called the House of David,
or if coaches once pushed you to ride a donkey
in a stunt to fill the grandstands on the day you pitched,
because when the Chattanooga Lookouts took the field
for an exhibition game against the Yankees, April, 1931,
you were on the mound, Jackie, the game ball
in your glove, signs given, chalk dust
marking the furthest limits of the field.

And no matter what blue streak he gave the ump,
no matter what dismissive quote he offered the dailies
afterward, when Ruth failed to swing at a called
third strike—he was and always would be
out, the scorecard a witness to each pitch
that made it happen, each pitch that sent the Babe
slowly back to the dugout, Lou Gehrig to follow.

With each wind-up and release, you harnessed
the laws of motion, principles of kinetic energy,
velocity, the round globe spinning from your hand
in opposition to the planet's gravitational pull,
Aristotle and Newton and Euclid detailing the flight
of cork and stitched leather, the distance it traveled

measured not in feet and inches but in the twin terms
of respect and scorn, each strike in the catcher's mitt
a potential redrafting of the world's known boundaries.

Jackie, for one brief moment in the history of the sport,
you struck out the Sultan of Swat and the Iron Horse.
Seven pitches: One ball, six strikes. You set down two
of the greatest hitters to have ever played the game,
and watched them take the bench, fuming, their bats
made mute. And even if forgotten by generations to come,
Jackie—for one inning they were masters only of the air.

MICHAEL SALCMAN

The Duke of Flatbush

For Edwin Donald Snider, 1926–2011

We were five and six: the summer bliss
of Bensonhurst, its flowing grass in our noses,
dandelions waving their yellow manes,
the smell of dirt in the outfield.

It was only a name, *Duke*, a talisman
of greatness, repeated under my breath
each time I took a swing,
my softly rounded body sturdy on its legs.

Duke, Jeffrey yelled, as he lofted a pitch,
clapping when I punched my way through the air
and the Spaldeen flew
like a satellite launched in haze.

The Duke of Flatbush died today
and something closed. A tassel torn free
from a valve in my heart flapped like old laundry
in its gutter of blood.

My head ached. How many days had passed
from that last soft-toss session
to the morning I stood and fell at my bedside,
the virus lodged in lumbar number five

claiming my legs? A year later, I would partially rise—
like Duke—*my lightness of bearing couldn't disguise
my darkness of being*—like Duke living his life
in the shadow of Willie and Mick.

CHRISTOPHER BURSKE

The Ars Poetica of Baseball Cards

In fifth grade I fell in love with the tired, capable bodies
of second basemen already old
by thirty, utility infielders just one bad hop away
from being released; .237 hitters
who'd stare down relievers the way someone might stand in a
    highway
and dare trucks to hit them; Peanuts Lowrey,
Luke Easter, Chico Carrasquel, Dusty Rhodes.
By the fourth grade I'd learned to love the abstract
justice of names: Billy Consolo, Ted Lepcio,
the *o* bouncing at the end of their names
like a ball scooped out of the dirt between second and third,
and the catchers, Andy Seminick, Mickey Owen, Smokey Burgess,
Yogi Berra, men built, it seems,
to squat down. I could see the fastball, high inside,
concealed in the glove
of Mel Parnell, a man born to play with the Red Sox
the way some men are destined
to be shipwrecked. As soon as his dad named him,
Hoyt Wilhelm had to throw a knuckleball.
Warren Spahn, Junior Gilliam, Nellie Fox—
where else could I hold a man in my hands
and look into his eyes without him
turning away. I was as free to gaze at him
as I was to gaze into water.
Eddie Waitkus, Jimmy Piersall, Ed Bouchee,
lifted free of the messy exigencies of their lives,
the Mexican Leagues, Korea, a shooting, a breakdown,

a man's entire year measured in at-bats, singles, doubles,
    homeruns, rbi's,
and each man smelled of bubble gum, pink, sweet,
hard gum I'd chew
until the taste was gone and then I'd chew some more
out of pure loyalty. I still know Milt Bolling's weight
in 1954 (178), the color of Billy Klaus's eyes
(hazel). Sacrifice fly, squeeze play,
southpaws, Texas Leaguers, pinch runners—
I grew more and more indebted
to language, the tiny print at the back
of the Topps cards, the stories they told
in only a few words, those old journeymen
who'd fill in at any position, play not spectacularly
but just good enough to keep the game
within reach, veterans who stared off into the distance
because they'd heard what no one else had,
a door closing, a train pulling out.

RYAN MURPHY

from Poems for Pitchers

Dear Dontrelle Willis

Eye of the storm. Fernandomania.
Dontrelle, I believe I can confide in you:
I have not written a word in weeks.
I am occasionally afflicted by a laconic hysteria,
overcome by delusions of grandeur.

Like Hurricane Isabel,
built for its own obsolescence
we build our past to fit any myth.

Dear Greg Maddux

Frailty is its own form of dominance.
"We drove that car as far as we could."
Arbitration, there is more that binds us
Decade of futility, who could ever forget
Chicago? Pebble Beach in October?

You must put them on your back.
Two seam fastball, cutter, pitch counts,
petulance, sign of the times.

Dear Fidel Castro

We will build our past to fit any myth.
Scouted by the Senators,
rhapsodic as shirt sleeves.
Yellow hammer
Yellow sickle.
History is a poor eternity.
I am thinking of the cool shaded rooms of Havana,
the opulent ruin,
Built for its own obsolescence.

Hey, Coca-Cola!
Rain in the bottom of the sixth.

Dear Sandy Koufax

We threaten eternity with our monuments.
Hurricane Isabel works up the coast,
coastal flooding, property damage
mystic waterfall, yellow hammer.
The eye of it. Bonus baby, living in the far fields
the mechanism of
the pure delivery, built for its own obsolescence.
"We drove that car as far as we could."

CHARLES MANIS

In His Back Yard, Kid K Plays "Burnout"

Winters in Texas, he works his throwing arm into rope,
    gristly cord that stretches and seethes over bone, whips
the end of every throw that begins with a toehold

    in the turf, and the roughed leather gnaws his fingertips,
sears them with the last snap of the pitch, as the red seams
    vanish into the fastball's white-hot twenty rotations

in half-a-second, so fast it seems to rise before it smashes
    in the fence's links like the clamor of his rasping
core, his chest so wrapped in sinew, his head crowded

    between the knots of his shoulders, the crash-toward-first-base,
fling-across-his-body, hard-as-he-can-drive-and-then-some
    motion reshaping his bone, like that bowed-out strike zone

of mangled wire, the ball that falls to the ground, its cover
    cut to the cork, his jaw unclenching, the ball swallowed
in the catcher's mitt, a loud pop, a burst of infield dirt,

    the umpire's back-wrenched grunt of strike three, and the air
that pours into the space of that short flight to the plate
    drinks what's left of the four-seamer's three-digit heat.

WILLIAM MATTHEWS

Babe Ruth at the End

The press loved him, of course.
After one game somebody wrote,
"Babe Ruth was not able
to make any home runs."
How about Ruth's roommate?
Wouldn't that make a story?
So they asked Ping Brodie
and he said, "I don't room with him.
I room with his suitcase."
He was out eating ribs

or some bimbo. Earlier
he'd stood in front of the hotel,
the winecask of his upper
body furred by camel's hair,
a camel's hair cap aslant
on his head and his deft nose
sifted the night air for lures.
On those spindle legs he stole
in his first four Yankee seasons
fifty bases. This genial slob

and imperious infant had
a disguise for his stealth,
and, like yours or mine,
it was his personality.
No matter that he barely hid
his life: cancer, that savage

biographer, riddled the Babe's
ample, only, and supple body,
and at last he lay like a balloon
leaking air on his hospital bed,

and Connie Mack, baseball's
Calvin Coolidge, last man
to manage in a suit, came to see
the Babe, baseball's Teddy Roosevelt,
on his deathbed. "Hello, Mr. Mack.
The termites have got me." History
has held Mack's tongue as easily
as it loosed Ruth's. What would you
have said, if you were Mack, or Ruth?
Something you already knew?

NOTES ON THE POETS

FRANKLIN PIERCE ADAMS (1881–1960) was a humorist and sports columnist for newspapers including the *New York Post* and *New York Herald Tribune*. His best-known work, "Baseball's Sad Lexicon," includes the famous refrain "Tinkers to Evers to Chance," a reference to the rally-killing double-play combination of the Chicago Cubs.

JAMES APPLEWHITE (b. 1935) is from Stantonsburg, North Carolina, also the hometown of Buck Stanton, who had thirteen at bats for the St. Louis Browns in 1931. Applewhite is the recipient of the Jean Stein Award in Poetry from the American Academy of Arts and Letters. In 2008, he was inducted into the North Carolina Literary Hall of Fame.

J. T. BARBARESE (b. 1948) has published five books of poems and a translation of Euripides' *Children of Herakles*, and is the editor of *Story Quarterly*. As a boy he played organized baseball and its neighborhood variations (stickball, half-ball, wall-ball); as an adult he coached Little League for ten years in Philadelphia.

MARVIN BELL (b. 1937) was born in New York City several months before the New York Yankees defeated the New York Giants in the World Series for the second year in a row. The author of numerous books of poetry and prose, he taught for forty years at the Iowa Writers' Workshop, and served two terms as Iowa's first Poet Laureate.

AARON BELZ (b. 1971) is the author of three poetry collections: *The Bird Hoverer*; *Lovely, Raspberry*; and *Glitter Bomb*. He claims to play first base for the St. Louis Cardinals.

DAVID BOTTOMS (b. 1949), a second baseman in his youth, is the author of two novels, a book of essays and interviews, and seven collections of poems.

GEORGE BOWERING (b. 1935) was appointed the inaugural Canadian Parliamentary Poet Laureate in 2002, and was made an Officer of the Order of Canada that same year. Bowering is the author of dozens of books of poetry and prose, among them *Poem & Other Baseballs* and *Baseball Love,* a memoir.

CHRISTOPHER BURSK (b. 1943) is the author of ten books of poems. He has volunteered for three decades in the corrections system, and teaches at

Bucks County Community College. His favorite baseball memory is catching fastballs thrown by his daughter, who pretended to be the wife of Satchel Paige with a Big League career of her own.

KIM ALAN CHAPMAN (b. 1955) grew up playing pick-up games in the lot behind his house in the Detroit area during the golden era of Tiger baseball—Ernie Harwell announcing games featuring Al Kaline, Micky Lolich, and Norm Cash, and Detroit winning the 1968 Word Series against the Cardinals.

TOM CLARK (b. 1941) grew up in Chicago, where as a young man he ushered at Major League baseball games. He is the author of many books about baseball, including *Champagne and Baloney*, about Charles Finley's Oakland A's. His latest volume of poetry is *Truth Game*.

DAVID CLEWELL (b. 1955) smacked a triple that drove in the deciding run in the championship game of his tavern league instead of participating in his college graduation ceremony. As no pro scouts were there to witness his prowess, Clewell went on to write poems. He has published nine collections—most recently, *Taken Somehow By Surprise*.

BRUCE COHEN (b. 1955) is author of three poetry collections, including *Disloyal Yo-Yo*, and is a member of the Creative Writing faculty at the University of Connecticut. Cohen learned Willie Mays' basket catch from his father, a New York Giants fan broken-hearted by the team's departure for San Francisco.

STUART DYBEK (b. 1942), author of two books of poetry and five of fiction, recreated Willie Mays' back-to-the-infield catch in the 1954 World Series over and over as a boy, until finally, in a game, he lucked into a perfect deep fly ball. The memory of the ball dropping into his mitt remains like a dream.

JOHN ENGLES (1931–2007) received many awards for his poetry, and published a dozen books, including *Recounting the Seasons: Poems, 1958-2005*. He taught for forty-five years at St. Michael's College in Burlington, Vermont.

B. H. FAIRCHILD (b. 1942) has published five poetry collections, including *Early Occult Memory Systems of the Lower Midwest*, winner of the National Book Critics Circle Award. When he discovered, reading baseball cards in right field as boy, that Dodgers' second baseman Junior Gilliam shared his birthday, he knew that he was destined to grow up to play second base for the Dodgers.

ROBERT FARNSWORTH (b. 1954) has published three collections: *Three or Four Hills and A Cloud, Honest Water*, and most recently, *Rumored*

Islands. He began attending Red Sox games with his grandfather in 1961, the summer Yaz took over for the Splendid Splinter, and has been visiting Fenway from time to time ever since.

ROBERT FRANCIS (1901–1987) was the author of numerous books of biography and verse. He lived most of his life in Amherst, Massachusetts, and wrote frequently of baseball.

KEVIN A. GONZÁLEZ (b.1981) grew up in Carolina, Puerto Rico (like Roberto Clemente), and (also like Roberto Clemente) ended up in Pittsburgh, where he teaches at Carnegie Mellon University. He is the author of a collection of poems, *Cultural Studies.* Because of the far-reaching tentacles of WGN-TV, he grew up and unfortunately remains a Cubs fan.

LINDA GREGERSON (b. 1950) is the author of five books of poetry, most recently *The Selvage.* She is the Caroline Walker Bynum Distinguished University Professor of English Language and Literature at the University of Michigan. She has still not recovered from that harrowing moment in 1986 when Mookie Wilson's grounder rolled through Bill Buckner's damaged ankles.

SARAH GRIDLEY (b. 1968), an English professor at Case Western Reserve University in Cleveland, Ohio, is the author of three books of poetry: *Weather Eye Open, Green Is the Orator,* and *Loom.* Her baseball hero is Roberto Clemente; her favorite piece of writing on baseball is Donald Hall's "Pitching Forever."

DONALD HALL (b. 1928) was Poet Laureate of the United States in 2006-2007, and received the National Medal of Arts from President Obama in 2011. He has published seventeen books of poetry and many books of prose. He followed the Dodgers from the age of twelve until they deserted Brooklyn for Los Angeles. Teaching at the University of Michigan, he became a Tigers fan, during the years of Denny McClain and the 1968 World Series victory over the Cardinals. Since 1975, it has been the Boston Red Sox all the way.

BOB HICOK (b. 1960) is the author of eight collections of poetry, most recently *Elegy Owed.* He misses the old Tiger Stadium. ("Hello, Willie Horton, wherever you are!")

JOHN MEREDITH HILL (b. 1944) has published poems in many literary journals. A former batboy for the Davenport DavSox, a White Sox minor league affiliate, he lives in Carlisle, Pennsylvania, and Provincetown, Massachusetts, and is a professor of English at the University of Scranton.

EDWARD HIRSCH (b. 1950), a Chicago native, was a catcher in Little League, then moved to right field at Niles West High School. He played center field for the Grinnell College Pioneers. Despite his outstanding batting average in Division III, some people think he is better known for his eight books of poems and four books of criticism. He is doomed to be a lifelong Cubs fan, though he now lives in New York and serves as president of the John Simon Guggenheim Memorial Foundation.

JONATHAN HOLDEN (b. 1941) is the author of nineteen books across a range of genres: in addition to award-winning books of poetry, he has published six books of literary criticism, more than two hundred poems in more than eighty journals and anthologies, and more than fifty essays and articles.

ANDREW HUDGINS (b. 1951) is the Humanities Distinguished Professor in English at Ohio State University. His most recent books are *The Joker: A Memoir*, *A Clown at Midnight*, and *American Rendering: New and Selected Poems*. When he played Little League in San Bernardino, California, he wore Clete Boyer and Tony Kubek trading cards inside his baseball cap. The cards did not perform the sympathetic magic he had hoped they might.

RICHARD HUGO (1923–82), an acclaimed poet, grew up in Washington State, and served as a bombardier during the Second World War. In his memoir, he recalls playing for both Yankees and Giants in an imaginary World Series as a boy. He would play all nine innings of all seven games, making sure the Yankees won in the end.

ROLFE HUMPHRIES (1894–1969) was born in Philadelphia in a year in which Phillies outfielders batted over .400 combined. He was a noted poet and translator, who taught Latin in secondary schools for many years in San Francisco, New York City, and Long Island, before joining the English Department of Amherst College, his alma mater.

YUSEF KOMUNYAKAA (b. 1947) huddled around the radio as a boy with his godparents, Lo and Bebe, to listen to their heroes, Jackie Robinson and Roy Campanella, whenever the Brooklyn Dodgers were playing. He is the author of eighteen books of poetry, including *Neon Vernacular*—for which he received the Pulitzer Prize—*Warhorses*, *The Chameleon Couch*, and most recently *Testimony*. He teaches at New York University.

LOU LIPSITZ (b. 1938), author of three poetry collections, grew up within walking distance of Ebbets Field, where he often sat in the bleachers for seventy-five cents. He lived and died with those great Dodger teams of the forties and fifties, and when he played, he imagined he was right fielder Carl Furillo, throwing runners out at the plate. Once the Dodgers left, it was all over for him: It was like finding out about Santa Claus.

DAVID LIVEWELL (b. 1967) is the author of two books: *Shackamaxon* and *Woven Light: Poems and Photographs from Andrew Wyeth's Pennsylvania*. A frustrated Phillies fan in the 1970s, he was gratified to watch them win the World Series in 1980, and even more satisfied to watch them win in 2008 alongside his six-year-old son, the biggest baseball fan he knows.

THOMAS LUX (b. 1946) was born in Massachusetts and is therefore, by blood inheritance, a lifelong and devoted member of the Red Sox Nation. He is Bourne Professor of Poetry at the Georgia Institute of Technology, and has published a dozen books of poetry, the most recent of which is *Child Made of Sand*.

MARJORIE MADDOX (b. 1957) is the great-grandniece of Branch Rickey, the Brooklyn Dodgers general manager who signed Jackie Robinson. She has published many books of poems, including several about baseball, given readings at the National Baseball Hall of Fame in Cooperstown, and twice been a visiting author at the Little League World Series. She is Professor of English at Lock Haven University.

CHARLES MANIS (b. 1987) was born into patrilineal Chicago Cub fandom, though he's spent most of his life in Pennsylvania. An erratic defender, he fancies himself a feisty opposite field hitter from either side of the plate. His poems and reviews have appeared in *Carolina Quarterly, RATTLE*, and elsewhere.

WILLIAM MATTHEWS (1942–1997) published over a dozen volumes of poetry, including *Time & Money* (1996), which won the National Book Critics Circle Award.

GAIL MAZUR (b. 1937) is the author of six books of poems, including *Zeppo's First Wife: New and Selected Poems*. She is founder of the Blacksmith House Poetry Series in Cambridge, Massachusetts, and Distinguished Writer in Residence at Emerson College. Mazur has been a Red Sox fan since Ted Williams; since 2004, she's adjusted with wary stupefaction to their winning ways.

DAVID MCGIMPSEY (b. 1962) lives in Montreal. After the departure of the Expos for Washington, D. C., he finally followed in his father's footsteps and became a Yankees fan. He is the author of a critical study, *Imagining Baseball: America's Pastime and Popular Culture,* as well as a poetry collection, *Li'l Bastard*, nominated for Canada's Governor General's Award. He teaches at Concordia University.

BILL MEISSNER (b. 1948) is director of creative writing at St. Cloud State University in Minnesota. He has published two books of short stories, four books of poetry, and a novel, *Sprits in the Grass,* about a baseball field built on an American Indian burial ground. He plays pick-up baseball frequently with a rag-tag group called The Catch and Release Baseball Club.

KEVIN MILLER (b. 1949) is the other of *Home & Away: The Old Town Poems, Everywhere Was Far,* and *Light That Whispers Morning.* He played baseball at Shoreline Community College in Seattle and Western Washington University in Bellingham, before teaching for thirty-nine years in the public schools of Washington State. He lives in Tacoma.

LARRY MOFFI (b. 1946) is the author of three collections of poems and a number of books on baseball, including *Crossing the Line: Black Major Leaguers, 1947 - 1959* (with Jonathan Kronstadt); *This Side of Cooperstown: An Oral History of Major League Baseball in the 1950s*; and *The Conscience of the Game: Baseball's Commissioners, Landis to Selig.*

MARIANNE MOORE (1887–1972) was born near St. Louis, Missouri. For her poetry, she was awarded the Bollingen Prize, the National Book Award, and the Pulitzer Prize. She was an avid baseball fan, and on opening day in 1968, she threw the ceremonial first pitch at Yankee Stadium.

RYAN MURPHY (b. 1975) is the author of *The Redcoats* and *Down with the Ship.* His favorite baseball team is the Boston Red Sox.

AMY NEWMAN (b. 1957) has published four collections of poetry, most recently *Dear Editor.* She is the daughter of a die-hard Brooklyn Dodgers fan and is married to the son of a die-hard Brooklyn Dodgers fan. She teaches at Northern Illinois University.

CAROLE SIMMONS OLES (b. 1939) is the author of eight books of poems, most recently *Waking Stone: Inventions on the Life of Harriet Hosmer,* and Professor Emerita at California State University in Chico. Several years ago, returning from a joint poetry reading in Brockton, Massachusetts, she and poet Maxine Kumin stopped at a sports bar for the late innings of a Red Sox game, where she fell hopelessly in love with centerfielder Jacoby Ellsbury.

SHARON OLSON (b. 1948), a retired reference librarian, graduated in the same class with revered Stanford baseball coach Mark Marquess. Her most thrilling baseball moment was when, in an elimination game in the 1987 College World Series, Stanford's Paul Carey hit a grand slam in the tenth inning to beat LSU. She is author of *A Long Night of Flying*, a poetry collection.

LISA OLSTEIN (b. 1972) is the author of three books of poems: *Radio Crackling, Radio Gone,* winner of the Hayden Carruth Award; *Lost Alphabet*, a *Library Journal* best book of the year; and *Little Stranger*, a Lannan Literary Selection. She teaches poetry at the University of Texas (Austin). Olstein fell in love with baseball during a late '90s playoff game between Boston and Cleveland with Pedro Martinez on the mound.

ROBERT PACK (b. 1929), an acclaimed poet and teacher, taught at Middlebury College for thirty-four years and was named the Abernethy Chair in American Literature. From 1973–1995, he was director of the Bread Loaf Writers Conference. Retired from Middlebury since 1996, Pack teaches in the Davidson Honors College at the University of Montana.

ROBERT PINSKY (b. 1940) was born (and remains) a Brooklyn Dodger fan. While growing up in his birthplace, Long Branch, New Jersey, he attended games at Ebbets Field as a guest of the Long Branch Plumbers Association. His recent publications are his *Selected Poems;* the spoken word CD *PoemJazz* with Grammy-winning pianist Laurence Hobgood; and *Singing School*, a kind of poetry anthology that is also a handbook and implicit memoir.

JAMES POLLOCK (b. 1968) is the author of *Sailing to Babylon*, shortlisted for the Griffin Poetry Prize and the Governor General's Literary Award in Poetry, and *You Are Here: Essays on the Art of Poetry in Canada*. He teaches creative writing at Loras College in Dubuque, Iowa, and lives in Madison, Wisconsin. As a boy, he once lost a tournament championship from the bench in the bottom of the ninth inning—by catching a foul ball hit by his own teammate.

ELIZABETH POWELL (b. 1965) is the author of *The Republic of Self*. She directs the BFA in creative writing program at Johnson State College, where she is also Editor-in-Chief of *Green Mountains Review*. One of the early girls in Little League, she was a terrible centerfielder, and dropped out after her front tooth broke in half from a ball in the face. Now she watches the Red Sox with her son, a Little League pitcher who tries to teach her how to throw a ball properly.

WYATT PRUNTY (b. 1947), author of eight poetry collections, fondly remembers listening to Braves games on a wood-paneled radio as a boy; his favorite players were Félix Millán, Phil Niekro, Joe Torre, and Hank Aaron.

He founded and directs the Sewanee Writers' Conference, and is Carlton Professor of English at the University of the South.

THOMAS REITER (b. 1940) is the author, most recently, of *Catchment*. As a fifth grader he attended his first big league game, in Chicago, and saw the Cubs' Ernie "Bingo" Banks hit two home runs.

NICK RIPATRAZONE (b. 1981) is the author of *Oblations*, a poetry collection containing a sequence of dead-ball era baseball player profiles, and *Good People*, a collection of short fiction. His varsity high school pitching career lasted only into his freshman season, when repeated shoulder dislocations forced him to retire from the mound. His last pitch was a slow strike for a save.

EDWIN ROLFE (1909–1954) was a writer and activist against fascism in Europe and McCarthyism in America.

MICHAEL RYAN (b. 1946) directs the MFA Program in Poetry at the University of California, Irvine. His recent books include *This Morning* and *New and Selected Poems*. Until he was sixteen, he spent more time playing sports than everything else put together—especially baseball, and especially the solitary-fantasy variety, winging a tennis ball against his family's concrete stoop and narrating the spectacular game-saving catches he was constantly making.

MICHAEL SALCMAN (b.1946) served as chairman of neurosurgery at the University of Maryland and president of the Contemporary Museum in Baltimore. He is the author of several poetry collections. His greatest baseball memory is of a writer's softball game at Sarah Lawrence College, when he struck out Thomas Lux, a fearsome power hitter, while shortstop Billy Collins hectored them both.

JAMES SCRUTON (b. 1959) is the author of four collections of poetry, including the award-winning chapbooks *Galileo's House* and *Exotics and Accidentals*. A third-generation Cubs fan, he writes frequently—and often tragically—about baseball.

FLOYD SKLOOT (b. 1947) was born in Brooklyn, New York, not far from Ebbets Field, and moved away from Brooklyn the same month that his beloved Dodgers did. In 1966, he played leftfield and batted leadoff for a Franklin & Marshall College freshman team that lost all of its games. He is the author of eighteen books.

BRUCE SMITH (b. 1946) went to college on a football scholarship and had a tryout to play professional baseball, although he could not hit the curve or throw accurately to any of the bases. He is the author, most recently, of *Devotions*, a finalist for the National Book Award, the National Book Critics Circle Awards, and the Los Angeles Times Book Award.

BARRY SPACKS (b. 1931) has taught writing and literature for many years at M.I.T. and the University of California, Santa Barbara. He is the author of eleven poetry collections and two novels. He was a Philadelphia A's and Phillies fan in youth, before going on to a more mature love affair with the Red Sox.

JOSEPH STANTON (b. 1949) is the author of many books of poetry and criticism, and two on baseball: *Cardinal Points: Poems on St. Louis Cardinals Baseball* and *Stan Musial: A Biography*. He is a Professor of Art History and American Studies at the University of Hawai`i at Manoa, and a devotee of the Rally Squirrel.

KEVIN STEIN (b. 1954) has published eleven books, most recently the poetry collection *Wrestling Li Po for the Remote* and *Poetry's Afterlife: Verse in the Digital Age*. As a boy, he dreamed of playing shortstop for the Cincinnati Reds. As a father, he coached his daughter's softball and his son's baseball teams for twelve good, hot summers.

MAY SWENSON (1913–1989) was an acclaimed poet and translator, and the recipient of the Shelley Memorial Award from the Poetry Society of America, the Bollingen Prize, and an Award in Literature from the National Institute of Arts and Letters.

MELINDA THOMSEN (b. 1961) has published two chapbooks, *Naming Rights* and *Field Rations*. She finds baseball to be a view of life within a confined space, so she spends hours fascinated by its goings-on. On the other hand, it could be that the Yankees are just plain handsome men.

QUINCY TROUPE (b. 1939) was born and grew up in St. Louis, Missouri. His father was a star catcher and a manager in the Negro Leagues, and the first African-American baseball scout for the St. Louis Cardinals. Troupe traveled with his father in the company of stars like Satchel Paige, Larry Doby, Monte Irvin, and Roy Campenella. His many books include *Miles and Me: A Memoir of Miles Davis* and numerous poetry collections.

WILLIAM TROWBRIDGE (b. 1941) is Poet Laureate of Missouri. His collections include, most recently, *Put This On, Please: New and Selected Poems*. Currently a professor in the University of Nebraska's low-residency MFA in creative writing program, Trowbridge's Major League career ended early, when he was cut from a sixth-grade summer-league team.

BRIAN TURNER (b. 1967) is the author of *Here, Bullet* and *Phantom Noise*, and the director of the low-residency MFA program at Sierra Nevada College. He hits for average from the right side of the plate and can occasionally take a pitcher deep from the left side. He's most comfortable at the hot corner.

RONALD WALLACE (b. 1945), the author of many books of poetry and prose, is Felix Pollak Professor of Poetry and Halls-Bascom Professor of English at the University of Wisconsin, Madison. His father was a Cubs fan living in St. Louis; Wallace himself was a Cardinals fan. (Their father-son relationship was conflicted in many ways.) For his ninth birthday, his father gave him a baseball signed to him personally by Stan Musial.

CHARLES HARPER WEBB (b. 1952) is the author, most recently, of *What Things Are Made Of.* He teaches in the MFA Program in Creative Writing at California State University, Long Beach. He played shortstop and won a batting title in Little League.

JOE WENDEROTH (b. 1966) is from Baltimore, and grew up an Orioles fan and a frequent visitor to Memorial Stadium. He stooped to attending Oriole Park at Camden Yards for the first time last summer. Wenderoth is Professor of English at the University of California, Davis, and has published five books, most recently *If I Don't Bw* Mexico Community College in Albuquerque, New Mexico, hom*reathe How Do I Sleep.*

MILLER WILLIAMS (b. 1930) was born the year that Dizzy Dean, also from Arkansas, made his Major League debut. Williams has written, translated, and edited more than thirty books, including *Some Jazz a While: Collected Poems.*

PAMELA YENSER (b. 1944) teaches at Central Nee of the Isotopes, a Triple-A team. Her poems have appeared on the *Kansas Poets Archive*, at *Connotation Press,* and in *Antietam Review, ascent, Elysian Fields Quarterly, Fugue, Massachusetts Review,* and *Poetry Northwest.*

ACKNOWLEDGMENTS

For editorial support via Persea's internship program at the University of Missouri, thanks to Greg Allendorf, Anne Barngrover, Monica Hand, Thomas Kane, Kelly Kiehl, Jackie Land, John Nieves, Elizabeth Otting, Chelsea Reynolds, Ian Thomas (we miss you, Ian), Jadee Wagner, and many others. Much gratitude, too, to Karen Braziller and Michael Braziller (Persea's clean-up hitters), Rita Lascaro, Fred Courtright, and Daniel Okrent for their support of *Heart of the Order*.

Tom Clark: "Baseball & Classicism" from *Light & Shade: New and Selected Poems*. Copyright © 2006 by Tom Clark. Reprinted with the permission of The Permissions Company, Inc., on behalf of Coffee House Press, www.coffeehousepress.org.

David Clewell: "Heroes" from *Blessings in Disguise*. Copyright © 1991 by David Clewell. Reprinted by permission of the author.

Bruce Cohen: "Spring Baseball" from *Disloyal Yo-Yo* (Dream Horse Press). Copyright © 2009 by Bruce Cohen. Reprinted by permission of the author.

Stuart Dybek: "Clothespins" from *Brass Knuckles*. Copyright © 2004 by Stuart Dybek. Reprinted with the permission of The Permissions Company, Inc., on behalf of Carnegie Mellon University Press, www.cmu.edu/universitypress.

John Engels: "Night Game in Right Field" from *Recounting the Seasons: Collected Poems, 1958-2003*. Copyright © 2005 by John Engels. Reprinted by permission of the University of Notre Dame Press.

B. H. Fairchild: "Body and Soul" from *The Art of the Lathe*. Copyright © 1998 by B. H. Fairchild. Reprinted with the permission of The Permissions Company, Inc., on behalf of Alice James Books, www.alicejamesbooks.com.

Robert Farnsworth: "Night Game" from *Honest Water,* © 1990 by Robert Farnsworth. Reprinted by permission of Wesleyan University Press.

Robert Francis: "The Pitcher" from *The Orb Weaver*, © 1960 by Robert Francis. Reprinted by permission of Wesleyan University Press.

Kevin A. González: "Ground Rules at Isla Verde Beach" from *Cultural Studies*. Copyright © 2009 by Kevin A. González. Reprinted with the permission of The Permissions Company, Inc., on behalf of Carnegie Mellon University Press, www.cmu.edu/universitypress.

Linda Gregerson: "Line Drive Caught by the Grace of Good" from *The Woman Who Died in Her Sleep*. Copyright © 1998 by Linda Gregerson. Reprinted by permission of Houghton Mifflin Harcourt Publishing Company. All rights reserved.

Sarah Gridley: "The Minors" from *Weather Eye Open: Poems*. Copyright © 2005 by Sarah Gridley. Reprinted by permission of the Copyright Clearance Center on behalf of the University of California Press.

Donald Hall: "Baseball Players" from *White Apples and the Taste of Stone: Selected Poems, 1946-2006* by Donald Hall. Copyright © 2006 by Donald Hall. Reprinted by permission of Houghton Mifflin Harcourt Publishing Company. All rights reserved.

Bob Hicok: "Root root root for the home team" originally appeared in *The Gettysburg Review*. Copyright © 2007 by Bob Hicok. Reprinted by permission of the author.

John Meredith Hill: "April" by John Meredith Hill originally appeared in *Elysian Fields Quarterly*. Copyright © 2006 by John Meredith Hill. Reprinted by permission of the author.

Kevin Miller: "McNeil State Penitentiary Closes" originally appeared in *Spitball* magazine. Copyright © 2011 by Kevin Miller. Reprinted by permission of the author.

Larry Moffi: "Homage to a Vacant Lot" first appeared in *Elysian Fields Quarterly*. Copyright © 2003 by Larry Moffi. Reprinted by permission of the author.

Marianne Moore: "Baseball and Writing," from *The Poems of Marianne Moore*, edited by Grace Schulman, copyright © 2003 by Marianne Craig Moore, executor of the estate of Marianne Moore. Used by permission of Viking Penguin, a division of Penguin Group (USA) LLC, nd in Canada by David M. Moore, Esq., Administrator, Literary Estate of Marianne Moore. All rights reserved.

Ryan Murphy: "Poems for Pitchers" from *Down with the Ship*. Copyright © 2006 by Ryan Murphy. Reprinted by permission of the author.

Amy Newman: Excerpt from "While Sylvia Plath Studies *The Joy of Cooking* on Her Honeymoon in Benidorm, Spain, Delmore Schwartz Reclines in the Front Seat of His Buick Roadmaster" appears with the permission of the author. Copyright © 2014 by Amy Newman. All rights reserved.

Carole Simmons Oles: "Interpretation of Baseball" from *The Deed*. Copyright © 1991 by Carole Simmons Oles. Reprinted by permission of Louisiana State University Press.

Sharon Olson: "Running the Bases" from *The Long Night of Flying* by Sharon Olson. Copyright © 2006 by Sharon Olson. Reprinted by permission of the author.

Lisa Olstein: "Dream in Which I Love a Third Baseman" from *Radio Crackling, Radio* Gone. Copyright © 2006 by Lisa Olstein. Reprinted with the permission of The Permissions Company, Inc., on behalf of Copper Canyon Press, www.coppercanyonpress.org.

Robert Pack: "A Fan's Soliloquy" from *Elk in Winter*. Copyright © 2004 by Robert Pack. Reprinted by permission of the University of Chicago Press.

Robert Pinsky: "The City" originally appeared in the *New Yorker*. Copyright © 2013 by Robert Pinsky. Reprinted by permission of the author.

James Pollock: "Radio" from *Sailing to Babylon* by James Pollock. Copyright © 2012 by James Pollock. Reprinted by permission of Able Muse Press.

Elizabeth Powell: "At the Old Yankee Stadium." Copyright © 2014 by Elizabeth Powell. Reprinted by permission of the author. All rights reserved.

Wyatt Prunty: "A Baseball Team of Unknown Navy Pilots, Pacific Theater, 1944" and "Baseball," from *Unarmed and Dangerous: New and Selected Poems*. pp. 28 and 72. Copyright © 2000 The Johns Hopkins University Press. Reprinted with permission of The Johns Hopkins University Press.

Thomas Reiter: "Game Day" from *Powers and Boundaries*. Copyright © 2004 by Thomas Reiter. Reprinted by permission of Louisiana State University Press.

Nicholas Ripatrazone: "Box Joseph." Copyright © 2014 by Nicholas Ripatrazone. Reprinted by permission of the author.

Edwin Rolfe: "Kill the Umpire! from *Collected Poems* by Edwin Rolfe, edited by Cary Nelson and Jefferson Hendricks. Copright © 1993 by the Board of Trustees of the University of Illinois. Used by permission of the University of Illinois Press.

Michael Ryan: "Hitting Fungoes" from *New and Selected Poems* by Michael Ryan. Copyright © 2004 by Michael Ryan. Used by permission of Houghton Mifflin Harcourt Publishing Company. All rights reserved.

Michael Salcman: "The Duke of Flatbush." Copyright © 2014 by Michael Salcman. Reprinted by permission of the author.

James Scruton: "Ghost Runners." Copyright © 2014 by James Scruton. Reprinted by permission of the author.

Floyd Skloot: "Whitman Pinch Hits, 1861" from *The End of Dreams*. Copyright © 2006 by Floyd Skloot. Reprinted by permission of Louisiana State University Press.

Bruce Smith: "Devotion: Baseball" from *Devotions*. Copyright © 2011 by Bruce Smith. Reprinted by permission of the University of Chicago Press.

Barry Spacks: "The Catch" from *The Hope of the Air*. Copyright © 2004 by Barry Spacks. Reprinted by permission of the Copyright Clearance Center on behalf of Michigan State University Press.

Joseph Stanton: "Catcher" from *Imaginary Museum: Poems on Art*. Copyright © 1999 by Time Being Books. Reprinted by permission of the publisher.

Kevin Stein: "Baseball Arrives in Richmond, Indiana" from *Bruised Paradise: Poems* by Kevin Stein. Copyright © 1996 by Kevin Stein. Reprinted by permission of the poet and the University of Illinois Press.

May Swenson: "Analysis of Baseball." Copyright © 1978 by May Swenson. Used with permission of The Literary Estate of May Swenson. All rights reserved.

Melinda Thomsen: "Tossing the Bouquet" originally appeared in *Naming Rights*. Copyright © 2008 by Melinda Thomsen. Reprinted by permission of the author.

Quincy Troupe: "Poem for My Father" from *Avalanche*. Copyright © 1996 by Quincy Troupe. Reprinted with the permission of The Permissions Company, Inc., on behalf of Coffee House Press, www.coffeehousepress.org.

William Trowbridge: "Poets Corner" from *Flickers*. Copyright © 2000 by William Trowbridge. Reprinted with the permission of The Permissions Company, Inc., on behalf of the University of Arkansas Press, www.uapress.com.

Brian Turner: "Jackie." Copyright © 2014 by Brian Turner. Reprinted by permission of the author. All rights reserved.

Ronald Wallace: "Fielding" from *The Uses of Adversity* by Ronald Wallace. Copyright © 1998. Reprinted by permission of the University of Pittsburgh Press.

Charles Harper Webb: "Shadow Ball" from *Shadow Ball: New and Selected Poems* by Charles Harper Webb. Copyright © 2009. Reprinted by permission of the University of Pittsburgh Press.

Joe Wenderoth: "Aesthetics of the Bases Loaded Walk" from *Disfortune*. Copyright © 1995 by Joe Wenderoth. Reprinted by permission of Wesleyan University Press.

Miller Williams: "Catch with Ruben" from *Some Jazz a While: Collected Poems* by Miller Williams. Copyright © 1999 by Miller Williams. Reprinted by permission of the poet and the University of Illinois Press.

Pamela Yenser: "Summer Games" originally appeared in *Elysian Fields Quarterly*. Copyright © 2001 by Pamela Yenser. Reprinted by permission of the author.